BEYOND GRIEF

Studies in Crisis Intervention

BEYOND GRIEF

Studies in Crisis Intervention

Erich Lindemann ,M.D.

NEW YORK   •   JASON ARONSON   •   LONDON

Contents

Introduction

How does one write an introduction to a lifework that has in its own time directed the careers and the lives of numerous individuals, shaped a field, and contributed to the well-being of the total population? To begin, one must appreciate the life, as a prelude to the work.

Warm, thoughtful, creative, and quietly courageous, Erich Lindemann was a gentle giant. His scholarly and engaging manner was the disciplined and civilized container of an intellect and a spirit that wrestled with violence, prejudice, psychosis, with problems of mankind that extended from war to impotence, with beauty in birth and dignity in death.

My first impressions of Lindemann were gained some twenty years ago. It was 1959 and I was sitting with Lindemann and a group of other young psychiatrists around a seminar table. He was nurturing what was then largely a dream—and imbuing us with the excitement—of community mental health. My last personal contact with Lindemann was in 1970. Here the occasion was more auspicious, a ceremonial event, the dedication of the forty-second community mental health center that had been funded by the National Institute of Mental Health in the seven years since passage of Public Law 88-164, the Community Mental Health Centers Act. It was the Erich Lindemann Mental Health Center.

Lindemann had come up from his illness for that event and his presence radiated warmth and optimism. Several of his former students, who at the time worked with me at NIMH, had asked that I pass on their personal regards. I did so, and though the cheers of the crowd were still echoing and the aura of greatness kept some of the timid from approaching, Erich Lindemann received those greetings with focused appreciation. In response to my mention of one particular person, he expressed deep concern, and said, "He still hasn't recovered from his father's death. He has so much to offer."

I understood Lindemann to be saying to that particular person, to himself and to me, to all of us, that we must move beyond grief.

The memory of that particular incident sums up much that is extraordinary about this book—he lived it rather than wrote it. As Betty Lindemann notes, the need to communicate and share was an essential part of his lifestyle. I feel that the opportunity afforded through this volume for other than personal audiences to share in that communication is an extension of his life. *Beyond Grief* is a rare book in that one can begin at any point, reading either backward or forward. The papers contained here might be viewed as milestones along a roadway or, perhaps more aptly, as colors in a painting—an impression which is reinforced by the exceptionally vivid imagery that he used to illustrate his basic concepts. Only the reader's integration of chronological line, of imaginative spirals and creative insights, can yield the full and bold scope of Lindemann's work.

Given Lindemann's mode of living his life rather than

compulsively documenting it, Betty Lindemann's notes become essential for perspective. In fact, the very involvement of Lindemann's wife in the publication of this volume, her persistence, not to mention her familiarity with the man and her insight, elucidates a major paradox. Lindemann considered the Human Relations Service project at Wellesley his most important work, but here again, he could never finish the book that would describe it. It is fitting that Dr. David Satin, a close friend and colleague, will assume responsibility for that book, one that will not only describe HRS but against that backdrop will explore in depth Lindemann's contribution worldwide to community mental health.

The papers in this volume are at the same time broader and more specific than a discussion of community mental health per se. Collectively, the selections establish a ring of concentric circles that are necessary to understand the individual at the center, the proximate circle of significant others, and the ever expanding outer rings of friends, neighbors, and communities small and large that define and support the individual.

In such a context, it becomes apparent that the slings and arrows of fortune, whether outrageous or merely mundane, can strike anywhere, at any individual perceived as a target individual. Lindemann perceived this, and realized further than an understanding of persons and their responses to trauma, loss, relocation, and broader issues of culture-in-transition might be conveyed, through crisis theory and social supports, to meaningful strategies of prevention.

The chapters fall along a continuum from familiar to relatively unknown. The first, "Psychiatric Sequelae to Surgical Operations in Women," and the last, where Lindemann reflects on the meaning of life in view of his impending death, will provide fresh material for nearly all readers of this volume. Yet even the best known of the selections—for example, "Symptomology and Management of Acute Grief"—still have much to offer. Despite its having been read and studied by thousands of people who have entered the world of human science, the message has not yet penetrated the decision-making processes of national policy setters. This and the following chapter should be mandatory reading for all who deal with the special problems of POW's, from Korea to Vietnam.

It is this ability of Lindemann's to address the darker side of the human and social condition—aggression, hostility, and violence—that is so significant; it may very well be this that supersensitized him to less dramatic crises. During his youth, the social environment of greatest concern to Lindemann and his family was that of Hitler and rumbling, prewar Germany. Out of this foment emerged Lindemann's unusual synergy of professionalism, one characterized by an equal ease with psychiatric interpretation and physical perturbation, and humanistic concern.

This, in fact, stood out in subsequent years as the dominant theme of Lindemann's work: the ultimate intervention he hoped to achieve was the prevention of war, whether it be between two bonded humans or all of humanity. His search for the most appropriate recipe for intervention between individuals and among groups was extensive. Thus, he was particularly attentive to "the insights borrowed from social psychiatrists and anthropologists"; the grass seemed green in other yards, but mixing the seeds did not always yield the hybrid vigor that Lindemann envisioned.

Still, the process of his search was powerful and fertile. His contribution to the mass endeavor called community mental health, firmly rooted in clinical practice, was clear and elegant. I suspect that many readers will be surprised and stimulated by Lindemann's straightforward and commonsense use of psychoanalytic theory and concepts in his pursuit of effective public health practice.

Today, a tenet of community mental health, and of health

generally, is the concept of prevention; given Lindemann's enormous intellectual range and his historic stature in the field now recognized as community mental health, it is fair to ask what contributions he made to the elusive goals of prevention, particularly primary prevention. His thoughts are presented in the chapter, "Preventive Intervention in Situational Crises," a paper that he considered among his best.

Lindemann pursued the issue with creativity and a courage that was perhaps most evident in his honesty: "studies up to now have not been possible on a scale and level of complexity which would be required to establish conclusive evidence for the linkage between noxious events and subsequent pathology."

It is not surprising that Lindemann approached the topic from a perspective most familiar to him—he tacks toward preventive concepts through a review of his own and others' work on the "essential components of grieving." The basic thrust of his paper addresses the role of psychiatry in the general hospital and the HRS, integrating endeavors through crisis theory and the prognostic use of role concepts. Though the field may not have been prepared, Lindemann had the creative vision: "the general hospital of the future will be a center for the maintenance of health just as much as a resource for the cure of disease and the rehabilitation of the disabled," he wrote.

The influence of Lindemann's approach is evident as one considers the current activities of such leaders in mental health prevention as Dr. Steve Goldston of the NIMH in designing preventive approaches to the ramifications of sudden infant death syndrome (SIDS) and in dealing with the preventive mental health aspects of the death-and-dying interests of the 1970s. These problems are part of the human condition and are worthy of the concerted efforts of mental health professionals of every shade and hue. "It is perhaps useful to think of the field of prevention as being many little things, and not to think that you have to start right away by conquering schizophrenia," Lindemann said.

He devoted considerable attention to the role of the psychologist in prevention in community mental health, and he emphasized the necessity of research—"the most important function will remain that of research," a dictum rediscovered by the President's Commission on Mental Health in 1978. Other roles he assigns to the professional engaged in prevention activities include developer of crisis intervention programs, consultant to professional caregivers, and resource person for city planners and public servants in social decision-making capacities. In retrospect, these roles, embodied in any one individual, define something of a superperson. Unfortunately, Lindemann provided his successors insufficient advice on how to gain entre to the world of politician and public official.

Lindemann's awareness of the significance of public officials and policy strengthens his argument that the miscarriage of coping abilities justified the training and development of "social therapists." The rate of social change has increased since Lindemann addressed this issue and promises to accelerate even more dramatically in the future. That social change is the primary dynamic affecting both individual well-being and fundamental sociopolitical structure has been underscored by recent events throughout the world.

In the series of papers on change, Lindemann defines his view of the new role of social psychology in a manner entirely consistent with his earlier comments on the psychiatrist's role in an individual's life changes. He adhered to the necessity of diagnostic and clinical skills, but was fully aware of the importance of such precursors of disease as the grief reaction. And while he advocated the need for modifying roles and value orientations, he was, I believe, purposely ambiguous so as not to rigidify criteria for the new professional.

"Together with social scientists [the psychiatrist] will have to address himself to social systems, whether family, kinship circle, small group, work team, institution, or whole community." Yet Lindemann did not specify whether the role called for was that of captain or investigator. It may have been his own realization of the limitations of social therapy that gave root to his caution. When he considered the activist leadership dimension of this brand of community psychiatry—labeled "sociatry" by Margaret Mead—Lindemann appreciated the potential for troublesome fallout. Two issues that he cited specifically were conflict within the profession and competency to deal with the problems. When one looks at the "boundaries" dilemma of mental health and psychiatry, particularly in the late 1970s, the accuracy of Lindemann's foresight is confirmed.

The discussion in "Ethical Aspects of Culture Change" is broad in scope and serves to mark both the originality and the incisiveness, of Lindemann's contributions. Consider his comments on ethics and the development of knowledge. "Somehow, what I call the 'industrialization of science' has got into this competition among scientists. The profit in this chase is the prestige. And in our time, prestige is an important goal which one must often purchase at the cost of ethical values."

Perhaps the most important dimension of Lindemann's contribution to social psychiatry lay in the actual nature of his practice in his last few years. And it is significant that in the paper in which he most cogently describes his matured conclusions about psychiatry's role in a time of social turmoil, Lindemann shows himself to have been most firmly sustained by his "faith in the methods he had used with clinical patients."

In the end, it is the disparity between his boldness of vision, his deep concern with global issues, and, simultaneously, his extraordinary compassion for individual needs that under-

scores the significance of the Wellesley Human Relations
Service project and further illuminates Lindemann the man.
HRS was a virtual Manhattan Project of mental health, in
which he never doubted for a moment. One may question
whether he realized the resource gap between vision and performance; no question exists as to his pursuit of both to the limits
of excellence.

A truly prescient and predictive dimension of the effort was
the emphasis Lindemann placed on citizen participation. In
his design, the citizens of the community would contribute
substantially to a range of policy and practical issues that
ranged from choice of research problems to determination of
the types of services that would be rendered. In establishing
HRS as a neutral meeting ground for individuals, groups, and
agencies, Lindemann made mental health an authentically
participatory process.

As one reads of Lindemann's many initiatives, of his innovative and caring primary prevention programs for preschool
children, his efforts and interests on behalf of youth and adults
experiencing a variety of life crises and less than critical life
events, it becomes fair to ask, "Did he succeed? Are the programs still in place? Did they prevent as planned?" Lindemann
would approve of the questions and encourage the necessary
analyses, but I am sure that he would also be breaking new
ground, raising still more questions.

Lindemann himself would never have been fully satisfied
with the results of his work and that explains the paradox I
mentioned earlier—he was never ready to do the final write-up.
That would be a task left for others. Yet he did succeed. Dealing
with individuals, approaching preventive mental health activities step by step, he was able to influence systems and to
contribute to shaping government policies massive in their
implications for the improvement and protection of individual
mental health. It is difficult to say when his goals will be

attained; his most important contribution was perceiving the needs and setting the goals. For that, we are all indebted.

Bertram S. Brown, M.D.

Preface

Erich Lindemann never wrote a book. Endowed with extraordinary gifts of two-way communication with patients and with live audiences, he recognized in himself a strong resistance to writing for an unseen public. Nevertheless, when he realized that I was not to be dissuaded from my purpose of bringing together in one volume his papers related to mental health, scattered in various journals over a span of more than thirty years, he collaborated faithfully with the undertaking.

We began to work together seriously on this project in 1969, when the fatal outcome of his illness appeared certain. The main shape of the volume had been established before his death in 1974; the only significant addition was chapter 14, in which he discusses informally his reactions to the prospect of dying. I have introduced the papers with brief notes explaining the circumstances of their gestation. The introduction to Part V, Epitome, was written by Dr. David Satin.

The title, *Beyond Grief,* indicates that Lindemann's work was not confined to his best-known contribution—his exploration of the psychological and somatic effects of bereavement. This book emphasizes the progression of his thinking to include the variety of coping processes and environmental supports in people's lives, the community context in which human function and mental health intervention take place, the role of the mental health professional in preventing disability, and, finally, broad questions of social change and the part that mental health work plays in it. Hence the focus of this collection of papers is on the grief studies and their relation to his innovations in community mental health. A completely representative collection of his works would include his papers on rehabilitation, and those dealing with personality and drug effects. His habit of tape-recording his talks and staff discussions has resulted in a rich mine of primary source material, by no means exhausted in the present effort.

A brief comment on the arrangement of topics may be helpful. They follow chronologically the progress of Lindemann's interests and work and can be thought of as an expanding spiral with themes reappearing amplified, more deeply explored, and integrated with new experiences as part of a broader and subtler understanding of the lives of individuals and communities. To eliminate overlap and repetition would have been to destroy the unity of the individual papers and a true picture of the growth of his thought; thus, it seemed better to preserve them intact.

The Clinical Grief Papers (chapters 1-5, 1941-1949) are concerned with observations carried out in the hospital on patients suffering from the effects of loss, either of persons or parts of the body through surgery. Chapter 5 is transitional: it reflects the author's increasing interest in the contribution which the social sciences, particularly small-group theory, can make to psychiatry.

Chapters 6-8 (Part II, Community Mental Health) portray Lindemann's commitment to a new identity as a public health researcher. Chapter 6 (1951) is a theoretical paper exploring the dimensions of a community orientatikjbbs 7 and 8 (1949-1961) bring together reports given over a twenty-year period of the two main ventures which Lindemann undertook outside of a hospital setting: the Wellesley Project, which established the feasibility of a mental health program in a middle-class suburb, and the West End Study of the effed0dt IIcts of relocating an urban working-class population. Both efforts contributed to the refinement of an epidemiology of mental illness and to new patterns of prevention.

Chapters 9 and 10 (Part III, Professional Roles in Mental Health, 1956-1964) reflect Lindemann's concern with the transmission of his innovative ideas to a new generation of practitioners. In chapter 9 he describes how he introduced what were then revolutionary changes into the medical school curriculum and residency training. Chapter 10, a paper originally addressed to psychologists, constitutes what is probably his most succinct and detailed statement of the *crisis theory* which evolved from the grief studies and became the rationale for preventive intervention.

Chapters 11-13 (Part IV, Addressing Change, 1966-1970) explore the effectiveness of the therapist vis-à-vis social systems in disequilibrium. Chapter 11 deals with the interface between the medical profession and other community institutions and views social change as an opportunity to bridge some of the barriers. In chapter 12, the emotional and cognitive components of role transition, as revealed in the bereavement studies, are shown to be equally relevant for understanding the effects of the role changes taking place in the teaching hospital. In chapter 13, drawing on his own experiences with racial confrontations and student protest, he states the limits within which he feels a consultant should operate in order to help control the destructive aspects of social turmoil.

Finally, at the urging of Dr. Irving Yalom, I have added the talk Erich gave to the radiation workers at Stanford Medical Center, which shows him transcending the grief of anticipating his own death. (chapter 14).

A book does not materialize without the help and encouragement of many persons. I especially want to thank Drs. Irving Yalom and David Satin for their generous commitment of time and interest to the enterprise. Edward Gulick, Professor of History at Wellesley College, and his wife Elizabeth were responsible for suggesting a major reordering of the material. Gerald Caplan and Herant Katchadourian read an early version of the manuscript and offered valuable suggestions. Shayna Gochberg reviewed the chapter on the Wellesley Project. Beverley Simmons and Margery Burns were faithful typists, and Barbara Mohr contributed her bilingual skills in preparing the manuscript for publication.

I also want to express appreciation to my mother, Eleanor S. Brainerd; to my sister-in-law, Gertrud Lindemann; and to our children, Jeffrey and Brenda Lindemann, for their interest and comments, as well as to the many friends who insisted that Erich Lindemann's book should come into being.

                                        Elizabeth B. Lindemann

Acknowledgments

Chapter 1 first appeared in the *American Journal of Psychiatry* 98 (1941): 132-139. Copyright© 1941, the American Psychiatric Association.

Chapter 2 originally appeared under the title "Modifications in the Course of Ulcerative Colitis in Relationship to Changes in Life Situations and Reaction Patterns" in *Life Stress and Bodily Disease* 29 (1950): 706-723. Reprinted by permission of the Association for Research in Nervous and Mental Diseases.

Chapter 3 first appeared in *Annals of Surgery* 117 (1943): 814-824. Dr. Lindemann's original report, which contained fuller case histories, was edited by Dr. Cobb for inclusion in the volume cited. It has again been somewhat condensed for inclusion in this volume. Reprinted by permission of J.B. Lippincott Company.

Chapter 4 first appeared in the *American Journal of Psychiatry* 101 (1944): 141-148.

Chapter 5 is reproduced from *Human Organization* 8 (1949): 5-9.

Chapter 6 was presented at the Eastern States Health Education Conference on the Epidemiology of Health, sponsored by the New York Academy of Medicine, April 1951. It was first published under the title "Mental Health: Fundamental to a Dynamic Epidemiology of Health" in *Epidemiology of Health,* pp. 109-124, New York: Health Education Council, 1953.

Chapter 7 is based on excerpts from "The Wellesley Project for the Study of Certain Problems in Community Mental Health" in *Interrelations Between the Social Environment and Psychiatric Disorders,* pp. 167-186, New York: Milbank Memorial Fund, 1953; "Use of Psychoanalytic Constrants in Preventive Psychiatry, part 1," in *Psychoanalytic Study of the Child* 7(1952): 429-437; and "The Health Needs of Communities" in *Hospitals, Doctors, and the Public Interest,* ed. J. Knowles, pp. 271-292, Cambridge: Harvard University Press, 1965. Unpublished sources for Chapter 7 include the "First Annual Report of the Wellesley Human Relations Service, October 1, 1949, mimegraphed. "Social Science Aspects of Mental Health Programs," paper presented at the Annual Meeting of the American Orthopsychiatric Association, New York, 1951; and "The Human Relations Service in Wellesley" (with R. Bragg), 1964, mimeographed.

Chapter 8 is based on portions of the following: (1) "Newcomers' problems in a Surburban Community" (with L.

Thoma), *Journal of the American Institute of Planners 28(1961): 185-193.* (2) *Social System Factors as Determinants of Resistance to Change" American Journal of Orthopsychiatry* 35(1965): 544-556. Reprinted with permission, from the *American Journal of Orthopsychiatry:* copyright © 1965 by the American Orthopsychiatric Association. (3) "Mental Health Services Relating to Crises in Urbanization." *Die Begeghung mit dem kranken Menschen,* ed. A. Friedmann, pp. 75-90, Berne and Stuttgart: Hans Huber, 1965. Reprinted by permission. (4) "Mental Health Aspects of Rapid Social Change in *Mental Health Research in Asia and the Pacific,* ed. W. Caudill and T-Ylin, pp. 478-487, Honolulu: East-West Center Press, 1969. Copyright © 1969 East-West Center Press. Reprinted by permission of The University Press of Hawaii.

Chapter 9 is based on a previously unpublished paper originally titled "The Mental Health Service of the Massachusetts General Hospital: A Setting for Community Mental Health Training." It was given at an unidentified conference, probably in 1956. The description of the emergency ward program and the program for alcoholics has been added from two later sources: (1) "Some Recent Development in the Activities of the Psychiatric Service," November 1964, mimeographed. (2) "Sucht und Rausch als Krankheit," *Nuenchener Medizinisch Wochenschrift* 107(1965): 49, 2461-2466. Reprinted by permission.

Chapter 10 was presented at the International Congress of Applied Psychology, Copenhagen, 1961. It was first published in *Clinical Psychology,* ed. G.S. Nielsen, pp. 69-88, Copenhagen: Munksgaard, 1962. Copyright© 1962, Munksgaard International Publishers. Reprinted by permission.

Chapter 11 is an abbreviated version of "Mental Health Aspects of Rapid Social Change" in *Mental Health Research in Asia and the Pacific,* ed. W. Caudill and T-Ylin, pp. 478-487, Honolulu: East-West Center Press. Copyright © 1969 East-West Center Press. Reprinted by permission of The University Press of Hawaii.

Chapter 12 is a translation, approved by the author, of "Kultural und Gewissen," *Muenchener Medizinische Wochenschrift* 111(1969): 17, 1010-1015. Reprinted by permission.

Chapter 13 is based on two previously unpublished talks: (1) "Reflections on Community Mental Health," address made to staff of San Mateo County Mental Health Services, March 17, 1970. Tape edited by C. Haylett. (2) Address made to mental health staff, Cowell Student Center, Stanford University, Stanford, California, March 20, 1970. Tape edited by Elizabeth B. Lindemann.

Chapter 14 is an unpublished talk under the title "Reactions to Malignancy and Subjective Responses of Patients in Life-Threatening Situations" presented to the staff of the Radiation Department of Stanford University Medical Center, Stanford, California, February 25, 1972.

Part I

The Clinical Grief Papers

Introduction to Part I

The following five chapters are based on Dr. Lindemann's work with patients at the Massachusetts General Hospital during the period when Dr. Stanley Cobb was Chief of the Psychiatry Service. Lindemann was then in his forties and had already established a reputation as an investigator of the effect of various drugs on symptomatic behavior. His best-known contribution had been the discovery of sodium amytal as a "truth serum," or means of temporary relief from amnesia. Cobb had been attracted to Lindemann, who was then a staff psychiatrist at the University of Iowa Psychopathic Hospital, because of this experimental drug work. No one, least of all Lindemann himself, could have anticipated that in the space of the decade, 1940-1950, he would become known as the leading expert on grief reactions. Yet it is clear that this direction was determined for him by events early in his life: the grief that he shared with his grandfather over the melancholia and subsequent death of his stepgrandmother and the painful death of his oldest sister at a time when he was already a medical student and realized that her illness had been misdiagnosed.

It is perhaps also important to keep in mind that Lindemann's work on grief was done during the years when World War II had severed communication between the United States and its enemy, Germany—hence between Lindemann and the surviving members of his family. It is likely that he transferred the concerns about their fate from his own situation to that of his patients, around whom he tried to build a network of supportive relationships.

Although these papers contained in chapters 1-5 record a new direction in Lindemann's thinking, they also reflect his previous interest in measuring activity rates, particularly rates of interaction between two people. Furthermore, the Clinical Grief Papers anticipate the next phase of Lindemann's development, in which he attempted to translate what he had learned from patients who were casualties of the grief process into a rationale for programs of prevention.

Psychiatric Sequelae to Surgical Operations in Women

Dr. Lindemann regarded the observations reported in this paper as the introduction to his subsequent grief studies because they led to the recognition that "loss of a part of the body can constitute an event which produces a neurosis or a depression." They also drew his attention to the angry, aggressive component of grief reactions.

In another sense, the paper presented in chapter 1 was a milestone, signaling his emancipation from the expectations which up to then had governed his relationship to his chief, Stanley Cobb: "I was supposed to write about the effect of preoperative anxiety on physiological reactions to anesthesia and the operation, and in fact I wrote about the emotional reactions. I was to write a second paper later about the physiology and never did."

Careful studies are already available about the type of psychiatric conditions found after surgical operations (Abeles 1938, Amreich 1937, Aschner (1929), Cobb and McDermott 1938,

Ebaugh 1939, Ewalt 1939, Miller 1939, Preu and Guida 1937, Washburne and Carns 1935, Wengraf 1935). A new consideration of this subject must be justified by a new approach. Although we know a good deal about the more dramatic psychiatric conditions that immediately follow an operation, not as much is known about the minor variations in behavior that may ensue later, and the knowledge obtained from post hoc observations has not yet led to reliable information upon which to base a preoperative psychiatric prognosis. It seemed advisable to make observations in patients before the operation and to chose patients who did not present special psychiatric problems but who instead represented the ordinary type of surgical patient. By learning to identify patients with liability to untoward psychiatric reactions, we may be of assistance to the surgeon.

For some time "traumatic experiences" have been alleged to be responsible for a variety of abnormal psychiatric conditions. Their relative importance and the degree to which they actually damage the individual can often be inferred only vaguely. Surgical operations present a well-defined trauma, consisting of anesthesia, mechanical injury, possible removal of certain organs, and alteration of physiological function set up by the injury. All these seem to leave no obvious mark in the majority of patients, but in some we find a psychiatric condition that suggests that the operation was a "traumatic experience," in the psychological meaning of the word.

At the Massachusetts General Hospital, candidates for major operations are examined psychiatrically whenever their emotional state seems to indicate the possibility of an untoward reaction. Cobb (1938) has described a number of postoperative psychoses observed at this hospital and has pointed out that the symptom picture of such conditions is not so much that of an acute delirium with confusion and disorientation but rather that of a vague alteration in perception and mood, such as is often seen in the so-called symptomatic psychoses with pernicious anemia or in puerperal states.

It is probable that these reactions are related to the metabolic changes and to the gross alterations in autonomic functions which occur at the time of operation such as avitaminosis, toxic factors, tissue destruction and vasomotor effects. In the present study we shall concern ourselves with certain conditions that come on later, as the result of the changes that have taken place in the body, when the patient has left the hospital and is facing readjustment in social and emotional relationships.

PROCEDURE

Our procedure differed somewhat from preceding studies, in which patients with serious disorders who came to the attention of the psychiatrist were described and where the events surrounding the operation were reconstructed in retrospect. In our own investigation, we tried rather to become acquainted with patients before the operation, to assay the amount of anxiety and attending upset of the autonomic system, and, in a follow-up study after six months or a year to obtain mental status and psychiatric history from the patients so observed. In so doing, we hoped to discover (1) whether the amount of anxiety before the operation has anything to do with the psychiatric postoperative course; (2) whether patients appear in this group who ordinarily would not come to the psychiatric clinic but who carry their misery at home or see their home doctor, being reluctant to seek the advice of a psychiatrist for fear of being hospitalized; and (3) whether we would discover psychiatric symptom combinations characteristic for this group that would permit conclusions about other postoperative patients whom we meet in the psychiatric clinic.

It seemed wise to restrict ourselves to a fairly homogeneous

group of individuals at the outset. Therefore, we chose a series
of women not younger than twenty years old and not older than
fifty-five who had had abdominal operations either in the
upper abdominal cavity or in the pelvic region, who had no
psychiatric complaints at the time of the operation, and who
had no discoverable disease of the central nervous system or of
the autonomic system. We also excluded all patients who had
any postoperative somatic complications and selected only
those who had an uneventful convalescence and who were well
after the operation in terms of their preoperative complaints.
The operative procedure was the standard one used in the
surgical department of the Massachusetts General Hospital.
The anesthesia was uniform and was controlled according to
the rigid standards of the surgical department. A record of the
behavior of the vascular system during the anesthesia was
available.

The psychiatric work respecting these patients consisted of
the following: The first step was to conduct an interview
during the twenty-four hours preceding the operation. In this
interview, a history of previous adjustment and possible psychiatric illness was obtained, and an examination was made.
The neurological, autonomic, and mental status was recorded,
with special reference to the amount of anxiety and the expectations concerning the operation, either anticipation of relief or
dread of bad results. Such preoperative studies were available
in fifty-one cases. For the follow-up study, only forty patients
were available. The others were excluded because of postoperative somatic complications (three deaths) or because they could
not be reached. The patients were visited by a social worker and
were asked to return for an interview with the psychiatrist,
regardless of whether or not they had complaints. They were
then interviewed and asked about their state of well-being,
somatic complaints, and changes in their emotional adjustment to the social environment and to their husbands and

members of their families. Special attention was given to the question of sexual adjustment and to their own evaluation of the operation. Abnormalities in neurological and autonomic status were also recorded. In addition, a mental status was obtained with especial reference to mood, distortions of thinking, and alterations in perception. An effort was made to conduct the inquiry in the same manner as before the operation. Complaints were recorded as presented spontaneously, and clarification was requested only after the complaint was presented. We were careful to avoid suggesting complaints with the questions asked.

OBSERVATIONS

In the series of forty women whom we were able to study in interviews that occurred from ten months to eighteen months after the operation, we found twenty-five who had no new psychiatric complaints, who showed no change in emotional adjustment, and on whom the operation had left no particular impression. Nine of these women were free of symptoms in their preoperative life as well. Five, however, had psychoneurotic traits and evidences of emotional instability, and two had shown considerable anxiety before the operation. In two of these women who showed no essential change we nevertheless found the continuation of severe neuroses in which the personality makeup of hysteria and tendency to the development of somatic complaints without demonstrable structural basis had been in evidence. Two of them had numerous operations before entrance to this hospital and were demanding another operation at the time of the follow-up visit.

The fifteen patients who had complaints had a free interval of at least three weeks and then developed more or less severe states of discomfort in which sleeplessness, restlessness, agitation, loss of appetite, restriction in activity, and irritability were the most disturbing factors. Two typical examples are the following:

H. F., age fifty-one, was admitted on August 2, 1939, because of excessive bleeding with menstruation, a condition that had persisted for three months. She was found to be in good physical condition except for the presence of a cervical polyp. Biopsy was advised to exclude malignancy. When seen before the procedure, the patient was confident and almost cheerful. She thought of the operation as a matter of minor importance. She did not seem especially worried about the possibility of cancer, although her mother had died of cancer. She had no signs of autonomic instability. There was no history of psychoneurotic symptoms. However, there was a history of two periods of depression—one period at the age of twenty-one that lasted two months, following her separation from the only man in whom she was ever interested; and another depressive period lasting about three months in the late fall of 1938, when she found herself unable to cope with the expanding demands of her professional position. She had remained single and had no active sexual life. She had developed, however, some regret about not having children. The patient left the hospital three days after the operation without complaints, having been reassured that there was no malignancy. For the next three months she had no complaints, but then suddenly developed a state of severe agitation, sleeplessness, aversion to food, and the delusion or conviction that she had ruined her associates in the agency in which she worked when she had left because of the onset of her previous depression. She developed suicidal ideas and had to be hospitalized. When interviewed six months later, she was found to be oriented, clear, and in good contact. She immediately recognized the examiner and implored him not to leave the hospital because she was sure that he would be killed. She explained that she had not been able to eat because she was afraid that when chewing she might hurt people outside the hospital. She was markedly depressed and restless and still insisted upon the chance to commit suicide, begging the examiner to give her poison in order to remove her destructive influence from the world.

A much milder condition is presented in the second case.

CASE 2

Patient R. D., age thirty-nine, had a total hysterectomy in May 1938. At the time of her follow-up visit in May 1939, she reported that she had been well for about four weeks after the operation. She then became unduly worried. "Little things worry me no end. I am all the time worried about the children. I have them dead and buried any time that something goes wrong with one of them." She was sometimes afraid she might lose her mind. She had frightening dreams. Someone seemed to be chasing her and she was trying to hide; people seemed to be breaking through locked doors; she seemed to hear a baby crying. She was apt to break glass and china very easily because, "I sometimes have an irresistible impulse to smash something." With all this, she was able to do her own work. She had seven children and did her own baking, cleaning, and washing. She found that it was much better for her to be very active, "I feel best when I have a lot to do. If I have nothing to do I get terribly nervous." The condition seemed to be gradually becoming better and she did not feel that she needed any doctor any further. Preoperative observations: At the time of the operation the patient was rather frightened. She did not know exactly what was going to happen to her. She reported that she always had been "of the nervous type." Patient reported a preceding depression lasting about three months twelve years earlier, after the breech delivery of her second child, who was born with a deformity.

A survey of the incidents characteristic of this type of condition shows the following:

Preoperative findings. None of the patients showed actual psychiatric disease at the time of the preoperative interview. Fifteen patients had signs of previous emotional instability (dizzy spells, fainting spells, anxiety attacks, exaggerated irritability, "swooning at the sight of blood"). Six had definite previous depressions; thirteen had former operations, and, of these, two had a large number (four or more) of operations. The upper abdominal operations were cholecystectomies. The lower abdominal operations varied from simple dilation and curettage or repair work to total hysterectomy.

The patients' attitude toward the operation at the time of the interview varied from confidence and trust to outspoken anxiety. Twelve patients had manifest anxiety, others were evidently making an effort to hide their fear, and some were under considerable social strain.

Postoperative findings. Twenty-five patients showed no change at all. Two patients reported marked relief of former psychiatric symptoms. Both had lacerated pelvic floors and had had repair work done. One of them was much pleased over better sexual adjustment. The other had been frankly afraid that the operation might harm her in this respect but was greatly relieved that this did not occur. (This woman had the belief that she had had only repair work done, when actually she had had a hysterectomy.)

Thirteen patients showed serious disturbances of their emotional adjustments to persons around them. A characteristic type of behavior was a mild degree of agitation, restlessness, insomnia, and a preoccupation with depressive thought content. In ten members of the group who were distinctly depressed, observation disclosed preoccupation with thoughts of violence, which intruded into consciousness: "I'm afraid I will hurt somebody. I am so scared I will do harm to my little boy." Three women had difficulty in restraining a tendency to expressions of violence toward their husbands and children.

They were irritable and unable to control their tempers. Three patients developed undue worry about the welfare and safety of husband and children, being haunted by fantasies that something awful would happen to them. There were, finally, two patients who were absorbed in self-condemnation and the expectation of doom for themselves. One patient developed a severe disintegration of her behavior, refused food, had the delusion that other people were dying on her account, and became so seriously suicidal as to require institutionalization.

Almost all the depressed patients showed a tendency to recurrent dreams dealing with horror, death, and destruction. In three patients presenting such a condition, we observed preoccupation, not with the region of the operation but with sensations in the mouth, tongue, and teeth. Numbness of the teeth, a feeling that the tongue is too thick, a feeling of having to crunch something between the teeth, a tendency to look at the teeth in a mirror, worry that blood might come out of the mouth, and dreams of blood gushing out of the mouth were mentioned.

The duration of the conditions varied. The onset was from three to four weeks after operation. In two instances, the condition was still present at the time of the follow-up examination (sixteen and eighteen months, respectively). The others subsided within six to eight months.

We were careful to determine whether or not the operation had merely accentuated a preexisting condition (for instance, climacteric complaints). This was found to be true with one patient. In one case, the patient had a depression that was complicated by a subsequent grief reaction following the death of her brother.

Comparison of Preoperative Observations with Postoperative Findings. Four of the depressive reactions occurred in individuals who had had previous depressions. They occurred twice as often in pelvic operations as in upper abdominal operations. There was, however, no relationship to age, pre-operative anxiety, or social strain. A very severe agitated depression with suicidal ideas developed in reaction to a single dilation and curettage. It was possible from the preoperative data to check our impression at the time of the operation concerning the liability of the patient to untoward reactions after the operation. Our predictions, based upon the presence of anxiety and the history of recent emotional strain, preceding depressions, or symptoms of emotional instability, turned out to be correct in only eight of the thirteen patients who developed the depressive syndrome described above.

COMMENT

Our studies show that in thirteen of our forty patients who had no preoperative psychiatric symptoms there could be observed a characteristic type of untoward psychiatric reaction, resembling a state of agitated depression. This reaction was much more common in pelvic operations that in upper abdominal operations.

We had hoped that a neuropsychiatric survey with emphasis on the autonomic status, the preoperative emotional adjustment, and habitual ways of reacting to distressing situations might reveal valuable clues as to the possibility of postoperative psychiatric difficulties. One might expect that a person who seems well adjusted and shows no preoperative anxiety has practically no liability to postoperative psychiatric difficulties. On the other hand, a person who shows much apprehension in the face of the operation and whose life situation is difficult might seem liable to have a stormy early postoperative course. A person who anticipates the operation with a sense of promised relief might not be liable to any severe postoperative reaction, but persons whose type of information is such and whose anticipations are such that the operation threatens mutilation and loss of sources of pleasure might be more likely to experience a more or less severe disturbance owing to a state of frustration with irritability, restlessness, and preoccupation with fantasies of revenge.

In our series of patients, we encountered thirteen who showed the type of irritability, restlessness, and preoccupation with fantasies of violence that we might expect. We must, however, be clear about the fact that our criteria for predicting the occurrence of such symptoms were not present in five incidents of postoperative disturbances; of twenty-five patients who did not develop any psychiatric symptoms, we had expected postoperative difficulties in eight cases. The most definite indication for the possible appearance of postoperative depressive symptoms is, from our series, the history of a previous depression in a person who has to undergo a pelvic operation.

The symdrome described here is so characteristic that it seemed worthwhile to watch for it in patients in the psychiatric outpatient clinic. Once our eyes were opened, we were surprised to find that we were able to collect a series of 23 patients within six months out of a total of 410, who presented the same picture and who had had pelvic operations within the preceding two years, in close time relationship to the onset of the disturbance. Some of them were self-limited conditions; others had continued for a considerable time and the patient seemed to be "stuck in a rut," out of which she could not lift herself. Since the condition resembles an agitated depression and since these women were, for the most part, in their late thirties or early forties, the prognosis would, at first, seem rather poor. We felt justified in trying in the psychiatric clinic to interpret to the patients that their present condition was a direct outcome of a violent reaction of the organism to an operation in which they felt mutilated, that a rage response had been activated, that this rage response had to find outlets, and that their disturbing experiences could be viewed as awkward attempts at obtaining gratification for these primitive needs. We found that on the basis of this rationalization, ten of the women were able to attain considerable improvement in their adjustment.

The tendency to demand further operations, which we observed in two cases of psychoneurotic reaction type, has been described in studies of the various forms of hysteria, most recently by Greenacre (1929) and myself (1938). It is usually not possible to do much for these individuals through psychotherapy.

The various forms of postoperative depressions have recently been discussed by H. Deutsch (1942), who, in the process of free associations, obtained information from her patients after they had experienced surgical operations. She found insomnia, depression, and a tendency to dramatic dreams. She also noticed a preoccupation with the mouth and nose similar to that shown by some of our patients. She emphasizes that manifest anxiety before the operation does not necessarily indicate liability to postoperative psychiatric difficulties.

From our own studies, it seems that only a considerable amount of time spent with a given patient will make it possible to understand what such an operation means to her in her emotional adjustment. Only rarely will it be possible to elicit the complicated interplay of motivations and fears that serve as a plausible explanation for her abnormal response to the operation. However, more searching study of a larger number of patients will be needed to find typical patterns of response that may be recognized and handled successfully before the operation. Only then may we expect with certainty that a series of psychiatric interviews before an operation can prevent a subsequent untoward response. At present, we must be content to state that in this series we could not confirm the plausible assumption that the display of anxiety before the operation is an indication of probable later psychiatric difficulties.

From our study, it seems that about 40 percent of pelvic

operations in women may be followed by a condition having certain features characteristic of agitated depression, beginning about a month after the operation and lasting more than six months. The condition may be mild but, in some cases, may lead to marked impairment of social adjustment and even to institutionalization. In most instances, it will be necessary to carry through the operation in spite of this expectation, but by psychiatric interviews we may learn to identify patients most liable to experience serious reactions. And even if we cannot avoid the reaction, we can inform the family beforehand and, after the reaction has occurred, may be able to assist the patient by psychotherapy.

SUMMARY

A brief review of the psychiatric sequelae to surgical operations in women seems in order.

1. Fifty-one women, aged twenty to fifty-five, were given a neuropsychiatric examination before major abdominal surgery, with special reference to anxiety concerning the operation, history of former psychiatric difficulties, marital maladjustment, and sources of environmental stress.
2. Forty patients who had no somatic complications and whose convalescences were uneventful were reexamined after an interval of from twelve to eighteen months.
3. Twenty-five of these patients showed no change in their psychiatric status. Two patients showed relief from former psychiatric complaints.
4. Thirteen patients showed a picture of restlessness, sleeplessness, agitation, and preoccupation with depressive thought content beginning from three to four weeks after the operation and lasting more than three months.
5. The relative frequency of this postoperative condition

was much higher in pelvic operations than in cholecystectomies. It occurred more frequently in persons who had had depressive episodes in their former life.

6. The incidence of this condition in our series shows no significant relationship to the presence of preoperative anxiety, to sexual maladjustments, or to environmental factors as elicited in the preoperative interview.

7. Reliable predictions as to postoperative psychiatric course will be possible only after more detailed studies.

REFERENCES

Ables, M. (1938). Postoperative psychoses. *American Journal of Psychiatry* 94:1187-1203.

Amreich, I. (1937). Geistesstörungen nach Operation. *Wiener Klinisch Wochemschrift* 50:674-679.

Aschner, B. (1929). Über das spätere Befinden von Frauen nach Röntgenkastration. *Zeitblatt Gynakologie* 53:910-931.

Cobb, S., and McDermott, N.T. (1938). Postoperative psychosis. *Medical Clinics of North America* 22:569-576.

Deutsch, H. (1942). Some psychoanalytic observations in surgery. *Psychosomatic Medicine* 4: p. 105.

Ebaugh, F.G. (1939). The psychiatrist in relation to surgery. *Surgery, Gynecology and Obstetrics* 68:372-376.

Ewalt, J.R. (1939). Psychiatric preparation of the surgical patient. *Modern Hospital* 53:62-63.

Greenacre, P. (1929). Surgical addiction. *Psychosomatic Medicine* 1:325-328.

Lindemann, Erich (1938). Hysteria as a problem in a general hospital. *Medical Clinics of North America.* 22:591-605.

Miller, H.H. (1939). Acute psychoses following surgical procedures. *British Medical Journal* 1:558-559.

Preu, P.W., and Guida, F.P. (1937). Psychoses complicating recovery from extraction of cataract. *Archives of Neurology and Psychiatry*, October, 1937, 38:818-832.

Washburne, A.C., and Carns, M.L. (1935). Postoperative psychosis: suggestions for prevention and treatment. *Journal of Nervous and Mental Diseases* 82:508-513.

Wengraf, F. (1935). Zur Frage der sogenannten postoperativen Neurose. *Wiener medizinische Wochenschrift,* Feb. 29, 1935, 86: 242; March 14, 1936, 298; March 21, 1936, 323; March 28, 1936, 356.

Chapter 2

Ulcerative Colitis as Related to Changes in Life Situations

The first evidence for Dr. Lindemann that loss of a person can be related to medical disease came from his intensive work with ulcerative colitis patients, in collaboration with Dr. Chester Jones, an internist, and Dr. Francis Moore, a surgeon. It is often assumed that Dr. Lindemann's interest in grief reactions was first aroused by his contact with the victims of the Coconut Grove nightclub fire, which took place in November 1942; but this was not the case. It was the discovery of the role played by loss in the onset of ulcerative colitis that made him consider it necessary to learn more about grief. In February 1942, nine months before the Coconut Grove fire, he reported to the Massachusetts Psychiatric Society: "Psychiatric treatment for ulcerative colitis centers around the problem of helping the patient to achieve the readjustment necessitated by the loss of the love object, and of enabling him to find a new set of close relationships. Because of the characteristic difficulty he has in establishing communication, this process is necessarily slow, and the therapist must continually be aware of the danger of arousing more depression."

Chapter 2 not only documents the effect of emotional dis-turbance on a diseased digestive tract but also describes the complicated strategies required to repair the patient's shattered human environment. The deployment of therapeutic person-nel, including nurses, occupational therapists, and social workers, and the nonexploratory, role-assuming posture of the psychiatrist, are illustrated in the ten case histories which follow.

In cases of psychosomatic illness, interest may be centered on the immediate interplay of emotional states and observable alterations in the functions of a specific organ; or the concern may be with the total disease picture, of which the disturbed localized organ function is only a part in relation to observable changes in the life situation and in behavior. Our efforts have been directed toward clarification in 87 patients from the gastrointestinal service of the Massachusetts General Hospital. The physiological indicators were those seen in clinical obser-vation—namely, the state of the gastrointestinal system as a whole, including appetite, food intake, food utlization, num-ber of bowel movements, weight fluctuation, and the infectious process as evidenced by temperature alterations. The psychoso-cial observations included evidence of changes in the system of social interactions with persons of emotional significance for the patient, on the one hand, and of alterations in the mental status as evidenced during psychiatric examination, on the other.

In general, our observations confirm my own previous re-port (1945) and those of Murray (1930), Daniels (1942), and Groen (1947), that loss of security, especially the loss of another person of emotional significance, is frequently encountered as the crisis in human relationships which preceded the onset of the illness. Table 1 shows the incidence of a severe loss of this type in our present series of eighty-seven patients. In this table is also found reference to the fact that the rupture of a human relationship may occur not only as the result of death but also as a consequence of being rejected, jilted, or disillusioned regarding the partner in the relationship. The important common factor to all the situations mentioned is a sudden decrease in the rate of interaction, the rate dropping to zero in the case of bereavement by death and going to a very low level with altered quality in the case of rejection or disillusionment. The variety of visceral disturbances and the alterations in mental status that are encountered in reactions to loss, even if they are "normal"—that is, self-limited and leading to adequate readjustment—were reported in a previous paper (Lindemann 1944).

An example of our type of observation is presented by the following patient:

CASE 1

L. C., age nineteen, was admitted to the medical service of Massachusetts General Hospital in October 1946. She was a nurse who had returned to duty three days after the death of her father, whom she had nursed through a terminal illness. Twenty-four hours later, she developed a fulminant form of colon disease with severe diarrhea, marked inflammatory reaction, anorexia, rapid decline in nutritional status, frequent vomiting, and severe impairment of digestive activity that could not be compensated for by medical measures such as intravenous feedings, antibiotics, and sedatives. On the twenty-second day of the illness, when perforation threatened, an ileostomy was performed, but the patient did not improve, and she died on the following day. The autopsy showed the structural changes associated with severe ulcerative colitis, yet gave no clue to physiological factors that might have led to the disease. The previous somatic history had been that of an unusually healthy girl who had not been sick during her period of nurse's training.

Table 1
Ulcerative colitis
Psychogenic factors in 87 patients

Bereavement	
Due to death	56
Due to rejection	9
Due to disillusionment	10
Total	75
Loss of cultural milieu	2
Threat of psychosis	6
Hemorrhoidectomy	4
Total	12

The mental status of this girl showed a marked deviation from normal behavior and subjective experience. There was no evidence of normal grief at the loss of her father. She showed amnesia for his image; his picture returned only in dreams in which he still seemed alive. There was marked emptiness regarding memories, anticipations, or future plans and activities. There were feelings of unreality, suggesting a state of depersonalization, a feeling of loss of identity, and the occasional feeling of being another person, having partly the features of her father and partly her own.

The account that the patient made with great clarity and in a detached manner about the period immediately following the loss of her father was notable, especially in connection with the fact that she knew about the father's expected death but had had to hide the fact from him: (1) To her, as a nurse, the mother had

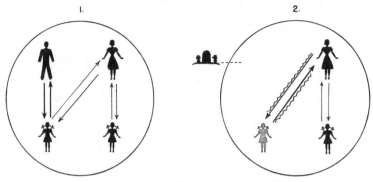

Figure 1

delegated all the errands and decisions concerned with the funeral; (2) a short period of intense display of anguish was cut short by the warning of a well-meaning person that she might hurt her mother by making her nervously upset; and (3) on her return from the funeral and the completion of her task, she experienced a process that she described with the words, "I froze up like a zombie." This state, which was interpreted by her as becoming like her father, continued throughout the period of observation. It was not possible to alter her mental status in the direction of normal grieving. Her condition remained one of apathy and detachment in spite of great intellectual awareness of the problem and a wish to cooperate with the psychiatrist.

Figure 1 presents a diagram of the crisis that occurred for L. C. A human orbit containing a father, a mother, and two sisters was replaced by one having only three individuals. It appears that our patient showed a reaction of great severity, whereas the other two women had the common signs of grief: crying, mourning, and preoccupation with the image of the deceased. The relationship to the mother, as the psychiatrist witnessed it and as it was inferred from interviews with her, was one of considerable hostility and apprehension. The mother did not approve of psychiatric help, being afraid that it might make the patient "nervous."

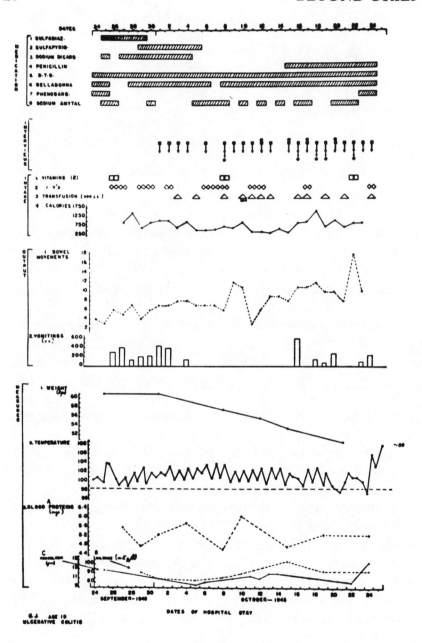

Figure 2

Figure 2 shows in detail the various efforts that took place during the period of clinical observation. The upper lines indicate the various medical measures that required contacts with the internists. Interviews with the psychiatrist are shown as black arrows. The reaction of the patient, as evidenced by the temperature chart, weight curve, and levels of blood constituents, is shown in the lower lines. This figure shows clearly that the interaction with the psychiatrist represents only a minor part of the human environment of the patient while she was in the hospital.

In the large majority of patients, it has been possible to modify the pathological grief reaction by psychiatric treatment with the procedure I have described as *psychological replacement therapy*. This approach requires (1) the determination of the loss encountered by the patient, (2) an evaluation of the special functions that the lost partner had in the patient's system of social interaction, and (3) an effort to use the psychiatrist or an auxiliary member of the ward personnel to replace temporarily and in a token fashion those special functions. Case 2 illustrates this procedure.

CASE 2

P. J., eighteen years old, entered the Massachusetts General Hospital medical service in June 1944, six weeks after his brother, two years his senior, had been inducted into the army. His somatic picture was that of a moderately severe ulcerative colitis with fever, impairment of digestive functions, anorexia, diarrhea, and progressive weight loss. He responded only poorly to nutritional replacement therapy. His mental status was that of perplexity, apathy, and lack of interest in any activity. The ward personnel complained about his whining, demanding, and dependent manner. The psychiatrist was called in to assist in efforts at making him eat more.

The psychiatric interviews showed a young man who was

SPACE BELOW IS FOR FIGURE 3.

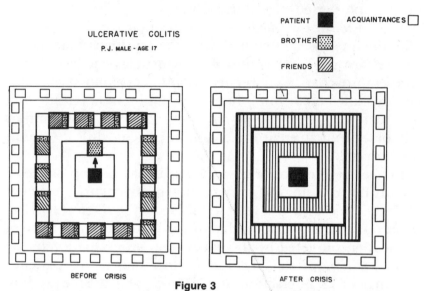

ULCERATIVE COLITIS
P. J. MALE - AGE 17

PATIENT ■   ACQUAINTANCES ☐
BROTHER ▦
FRIENDS ▨

BEFORE CRISIS   AFTER CRISIS

Figure 3

not looking forward to anything, had no plans or hopes, felt apathetic and empty without being able to account for it, and had a vague sense of impending doom. In an objective, detached manner, he reported about his brother's leaving for the army and in the course of subsequent discussions described, without any awareness of a painful loss, how he had always tagged along with his brother, how his brother had initiated all his social activities, and how he had no friends of his own but had shared his brother's friends; he said, "I even shared his girlfriend." A detailed analysis of his set of human relationships showed that at present he did not consider anybody an intimate friend with whom he could share personal matters and that all those young people with whom he used to spend time and enjoy activities before his brother's departure seemed to have become strangers to him.

Figure 3 diagrams the social system which the patient in case 2 described. In the left-hand figure, the patient is seen in the

ULCERATIVE COLITIS P. J.

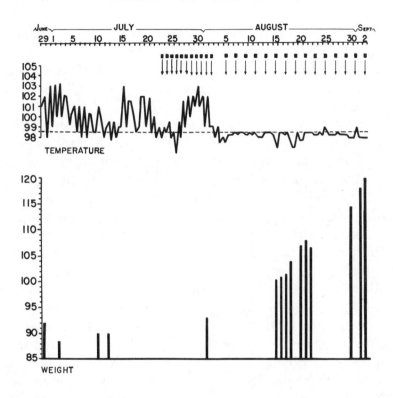

PSYCHIATRIC INTERVIEW = █

Figure 4

center of three concentric squares. The first one shows intimate relationships of the first order and great emotional significance; the second, those relationships providing opportunity for shared activities; and the third, those of casual acquaintance. It became quite clear that for P. J., the departure of the brother had produced the condition illustrated by the right-hand figure. The brother's absence had resulted in multiple bereavement, leaving him without activities, and opportunities for shared activity and laying bare his own inability to initiate social interaction. The brother had served as an avenue of access to other individuals and had been the initiator of joint activities.

Figure 4 provides a simplified diagram of the clinical course of the patient's condition, presenting evidence of the return of the temperature to normal and an increase in weight as a consequence of improved appetite after several psychiatric interviews.

The substitution therapy based on an evaluation of the life situation had consisted of an effort to provide a token experience of shared activity with the therapist, such as could be given by having the patient read certain books that the therapist also had been reading and discussing them with him and by suggesting that he also acquire skills such as typewriting and describing to him the therapist's own struggles to acquire this technique. The other line of approach was a systematic ritual of introducing the patient to a number of the people in the ward whom the therapist already knew, so that the therapist also became an avenue of access to other individuals with whom to share activities. The patient rapidly accepted the transfer to the therapist of the role previously carried by the brother. The change in his somatic condition was accompanied by a marked change in mental status, with active planning for the future in terms of an occupation that presumably might be of interest to the therapist and with rapidly expanding interest in various kinds of ward activities.

After four months, the patient's brother returned from the service, and the equilibrium that had preceded the crisis in the patient's life situation was reestablished. The brother has since permitted the patient to stay in a somewhat dependent relationship to him, and there has been no recurrence of his colon disease. P. J. must, however, be considered a vulnerable individual subject to further somatic symptoms should a new separation occur.

We consider the form of replacement therapy used with case 2, aimed at reestablishing an equilibrium of social relations that has been lost, an emergency phase of psychiatric management. Whenever possible, this emergency therapy should be followed by efforts to alter the patient's personality in such a way that he may be rendered less vulnerable to renewed loss.

Active manipulation of the life situation, as represented by the pattern of interaction with other individuals of emotional significance to the patient, is relatively easy wherever the roles played for each other by the various partners of the social system are clearly understood. Difficulties may arise, however, if the patient's expectations of a partner he has recently lost or those to which he feels entitled are such that they cannot readily be replaced. Such a situation is illustrated by case 3.

CASE 3

F. A., a sixteen-year-old boy, was admitted to the medical service of the Massachusetts General Hospital in April 1946 with moderately severe ulcerative colitis, which had developed two years before when a brother, two years older, had been drafted. The patient had reacted to this loss with withdrawal from all companionship with other boys and a loss of interest in his former activities. When the psychiatrist tried to review the role that the boy's brother had played in his life, it was found that the patient felt secure only when his strong brother was available to fight off other boys who might attack him. After a few interviews, the patient reenacted on the ward his demands for evidence that the therapist had power to protect him. He provoked other patients on the ward to aggressive behavior and wished the therapist to be called to defend him.

F. A. soon extended his provocative behavior to the ward personnel and to the ward visitor, being utterly disappointed and discouraged when it turned out to be impossible for the therapist to protect him from his "adversaries," as he called them, by the sort of dramatic encounter he wished to witness.

His preoccupation with the aggressive interest in him of other boys and men, which had a paranoid coloring, was not open to analysis and control, and, in view of this situation, little progress was made in relieving the abnormal colon condition.

Once the therapist has assumed the role of becoming an obligatory person in the patient's human orbit, the patient is likely to become vulnerable to the therapist's departure or to any attempts at premature termination of the period of treatment, as evidenced by case 4.

CASE 4

A nineteen-year-old boy, D. F., had developed a moderately severe form of ulcerative colitis after his father was removed from his social orbit by being jailed for an immoral act, an occurrence that was extremely disillusioning to the patient. The house officer on the psychiatric service, as well as the visiting psychiatrist, developed a supportive relationship to this boy, offering him interaction with a reliable person whose character he learned to trust. Although the therapist had some misgivings about the possible consequences, after careful discussion with the patient, who intellectually accepted the change as inevitable, both physicians departed according to their scheduled plans; the house officer had finished his service and moved on to another appointment, and the psychiatrist left for a month's vacation. The patient showed no outward emotion in connection with this double loss, but within three days following departure of both physicians, he developed a severe exacerbation of his illness and required an ileostomy. Figures 5 and 6 present his temperature and weight charts.

The occurrence of a severe loss and the absence of an adequate emotional response to the loss in the form of a grief reaction

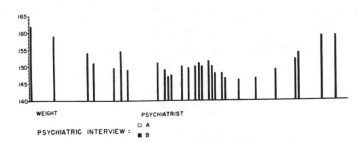

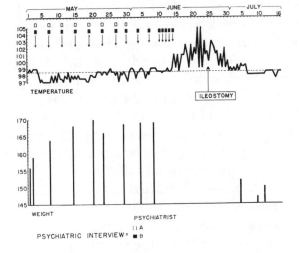

Figure 5

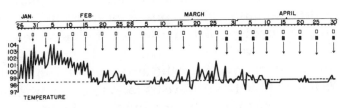

Figure 6

as evidenced by mental status and history are of equal importance in the evaluation of an episode of ulcerative colitis. Of special interest is a type of delayed reaction that occurs when a patient, after a severe loss, is removed to an entirely new environment in which there is little to remind him of the loss encountered and then returns years later to an environment of similar social structure as the one in which the loss occurred. Such a return may become the precipitating crisis that looms up in the most recent history, and only in the course of the subsequent investigation of the patient may the gravity of the loss be recognized and the reaction to it become manifest. This sequence of events is illustrated by case 5.

CASE 5

J. H. was admitted at age seventeen to the medical service with a severe form of ulcerative colitis. Her condition had developed about a month after she had been placed by a social agency in a foster home, where she was expected to earn her way by domestic service. She had been transferred to this home from an institution in which she had spent four years with other adolescent girls under the supervision of matrons. Her care in this institution had been decided upon by the social agency after the mother deserted the family when the patient was thirteen years old. At that time, the father was not considered able to take care of the children, and her siblings were placed in various other institutions. The patient had communicated with her father only through rare letters and had no knowledge of the whereabouts of the other children.

When the patient was admitted to the ward, she appeared cheerful, restless, somewhat overactive, and was annoying to the house officer because of her unwillingness to stay in bed. She denied any concern about the members of her family and maintained that her mother had died about five years before but that this did not make any difference to her. She showed considerable resentment whenever the subject of her own family was brought up for discussion.

The management of both life situation and emotional response required, as the therapist saw it, sufficient replacement therapy employing both a maternal and a paternal figure to reduce the severity of the emotional response that might follow if a grief process were to be precipitated. At the same time, it seemed necessary to see the patient, under the protection of the ward environment, through a process of mourning for her mother before any reduction of emotional tension could be expected. During the period of discussion of the original family setup, which followed a detailed account of the present foster home, the patient recognized how similar her feelings in her present home were to those connected with her own family years before. She became severely depressed and anxious, experienced a sense of loss and hopelessness, and showed considerable bitterness toward the social workers, who she now felt were responsible for having deprived her of the members of her family. With the help of the social agencies, contact by letter was reestablished with her siblings, and the prospect of being reunited with her father and caring for him and at least one or two of her siblings was discussed. The patient's ulcerative colitis condition rapidly improved. She returned to her foster home, but after a week ran away from it, found her father in a distant village, and started keeping house for him. There has been no exacerbation of the disease since then.

Figure 7 shows in diagram form the structure of the social orbit before the crisis produced by the mother's departure and the consequence to the patient's orbit of human relations. It also shows the structure of the family orbit in the foster home and of the institution, where the context of human relations markedly differed from that of a typical family system. Figure 8 shows the number of bowel movements on day-by-day counts

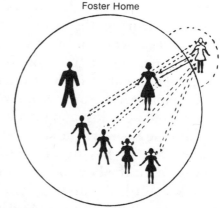

Figure 7

during the period of psychiatric therapy. The marked increase in the rate of bowel movements during the period of discussion of the loss will be noticed. On the twenty-first day, the social worker responsible for the patient, against whom she was so bitter, visited the hospital; there was a severe outburst of anger against this woman not followed by any apparent increase in the number of bowel movements. Figure 9 shows (a) the pattern of social interactions when the patient had gained the support of the psychiatrist and hospital social worker, and (b) the structure of the final social orbit in which she again was in relative emotional equilibrium.

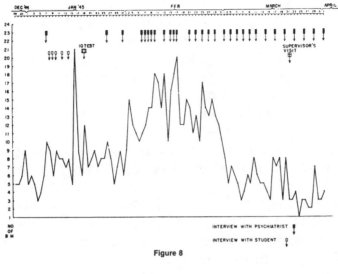

Figure 8

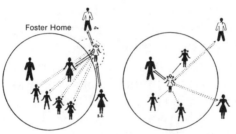

Figure 9

The constellation of the human environment, which is required by a patient with ulcerative colitis if he is to avoid new episodes of his illness, is illustrated by two examples—cases 6 and 7.

CASE 6

A nineteen-year-old boy, H. T., was admitted to the medical wards of the Massachusetts General Hospital in a state of fairly severe bowel disturbance approximately a year after the onset of his illness. The psychiatric study showed that the onset followed shortly after his leaving high school. His emotionally relevant human environment had consisted of two boys somewhat older than he was and to whom he was very much attached. For H. T., these two boys were models for activity and initiators of shared action; one of them had gone to college, and the other had left the country.

The patient was followed for five years and was seen during six major fluctuations in his illness. During the first year of observation, he married but showed no improvement in his condition. During the second year, he developed a friendship with a male instructor during a summer course at the university. He developed a close companionship with this man and devoted himself to studies in the field in which the latter was competent. At this time, the patient was free of symptoms; he had normal bowel movements and marked weight gain during the period of the duration of this friendship. He returned with an exacerbation of his symptoms when the instructor left at the end of the summer. There was another period of improvement during the following summer, when the male instructor returned to work in the vicinity and renewed a period of close companionship. The patient experienced a return to moderately severe illness after his friend left.

In the following year the patient obtained a divorce from his wife and remarried. His second wife was a woman with strong intellectual ambitions and a rather aggressive, domineering manner; she permitted him a considerable degree of dependence and initiated most of their joint planning. The patient's state of health improved markedly after his remarriage.

The person whose presence in the orbit of human relationships is indispensable for the patient may well be an individual who becomes conspicuous in his role only in the course of a careful analysis of the system of human relationships. A friend or relative of one of the parents who lives within the family

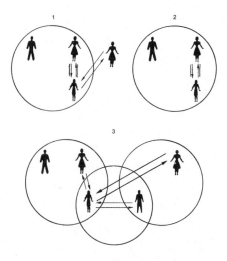

Figure 10

orbit and becomes the object of affectionate and authoritarian systems of interactions may, by his departure, cause a severe grief reaction, which takes the form of an episode of ulcerative colitis; as in case 7.

CASE 7

Figure 10 illustrates the orbit of human relations of case 7. The initial orbit (Diagram 1) includes a father, mother, and an eighteen-year-old daughter, a high-school graduate, as well as a woman friend of the mother's to whom the latter was very much attached. The initial orbit was replaced when the mother's woman friend married by the orbit presented in Diagram 2, which contains only the family. Within six weeks after this event, the young girl developed ulcerative colitis, which rapidly progressed to a severe state of malnutrition, accompanied by confusion and hallucinatory experiences.

In the course of the psychiatric investigation, it became clear that the daughter had been an unwanted child, whose birth had forced the father and mother, who were college students at the time of the conception, to marry and, as a result, to experience a strong sense of guilt and disgrace. The mother gave up her wish to become a professional woman in atonement for her guilt; after three years of retirement and hiding, the father returned to college to finish his academic work. The marriage had remained precarious. The husband had developed a gastric ulcer and had anxiety attacks with fainting spells. After the departure of the mother's friend, the mother showed outspoken hostility to the young girl, and one of the patient's recurring fantasies was that her mother wanted to kill her. The patient's initial improvement coincided with the development of a strong attachment to a nurse in the hospital, and there was a return of moderately severe colon disturbance when she left the hospital to be cared for by her mother.

After a year and a half without any marked changes in her condition, the patient became very much attached to a middle-aged woman, whose son she subsequently married. Since the development of this relationship, her somatic condition has been excellent, and she has even survived pregnancy and the delivery of her first child without any exacerbation of her colon disturbance. She has come to recognize the obligatory nature of the relationship to her mother-in-law and has accepted the necessity of such a close emotional dependence. Diagram 3 illustrates the three family orbits: of both marriage partners and that of the new family of procreation of which the patient's mother-in-law is an important partner.

From the point of view of the requirements of human relationships of patients with ulcerative colitis, it is of some interest that fluctuations in the well-being of other members of the family may coincide with exacerbations and remissions in the condition of the ulcerative colitis patient. This is illustrated by cases 8 and 9.

CASE 8

H. S., a girl twelve years of age, was admitted to the children's medical service of the Massachusetts General Hospital in a severe state of ulcerative colitis. The condition had developed two months before, while she was in a sanitarium for rheumatic heart disease suspects. At that time, she had complained of heart pounding and weakness and was considered in need of observation. Her entrance into the sanitarium had removed her from the family orbit. The family had consisted of the patient, her father, her mother, and a brother. There also had been an additional person of great importance, the mother's brother. This man had died of a gastrointestinal illness about five weeks before the onset of the girl's heart symptoms. The mother had developed a severe mourning reaction with intense preoccupation with the deceased and markedly reduced interaction with the patient, who was extremely dependent on her. The patient had developed an attachment to her brother, and had been rejected by him when she always tried to tag along. She was removed from the family altogether by being taken to the sanitarium, and she soon developed hostility and provocative behavior toward the head nurse. The authorities of the sanitarium finally requested that she be taken home because of her misbehavior; but just before her discharge, she began to show bloody diarrhea with fever and was transferred with a diagnosis of ulcerative colitis to the Massachusetts General Hospital.

On the children's service she found a tolerant nurse and a boy patient, who permitted her to copy his activities and join him in modeling and painting. The patient soon became aware of a great gift for drawing and painting and showed a marked improvement in her colon condition. She was discharged to her

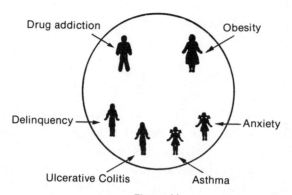

Figure 11

home as much improved, but she returned to the same orbit of human relationships that had originally disturbed her. After two months, she was readmitted because of a severe exacerbation. Efforts were made to help the mother toward a normal grief reaction in response to the loss of her brother. The mother then became attached to a male patient with ulcerative colitis whom she met in the hospital, and she showed a similar amount of concern and interest in him as she previously had shown in regard to her brother. Her attitude toward the little girl became more relaxed and accepting, and there followed a gradual improvement in the child's condition.

CASE 9

When first seen, the patient was thirteen years old and was suffering from ulcerative colitis. She was one of four girls. The oldest, age seventeen, was considered a sexual delinquent; the sister next to her, age eleven, was considered to have moderate asthma; and the youngest, age eight, had severe attacks of anxiety and a school phobia. This social orbit is illustrated by Figure 11.

The patient was seen through four major exacerbations in the severity of her disease, as indicated by changes in weight, number of bowel movements, and evidence of active infection.

Each of these started with extreme concern about her father, who, supposedly unknown to the children, was a cocaine addict and who developed episodes of inefficiency and apparent preoccupation at the times of intensified addiction. At these occasions, the mother was much concerned about the father. The recurrent picture in the child's mind was that of visualizing her father in a train or plane accident and herself coming too late to rescue him.

A final example of the time relationship between marked fluctuations in the disease picture and the life situation is provided by Case 10.

CASE 10

This boy was first seen at the age of eleven, and he was followed for four years. During the first two years he had four severe exacerbations of his illness, which had a clear time relationship to the development of depressive mood disturbances in his mother. During the period in which the mother was without depression, there existed a fairly intense interplay of mutually aggressive behavior, the mother being anxious to restrict the child's high rate of activity and, because of overprotective needs, restraining him from participation in many activities with other children to which he felt entitled. When the mother became depressed, her activity rate became markedly lessened. She was preoccupied and showed little apparent interest in the patient.

The boy developed the fantasy that she might drown or be killed by a dangerous man. He felt haunted by such thoughts and felt guilty about them. A mild state of depressive mood, apathy, and much reduced activity, with a tendency to stay home to watch his mother, preceded by a week first the onset and later the recurrence of a severe bowel disturbance with ulcerative changes. The disturbances of the mother were analyzed psychiatrically and found to be a series of reactive depressions linked to fluctuations of interaction with women friends, who were indispensable to her if she was to maintain emotional equilibrium in an unsatisfactory marriage.

ULCERATIVE COLITIS AND PSYCHOTIC MANIFESTATIONS

Several of the examples mentioned have referred to mental disturbances encountered at the time of an attack of ulcerative colitis. We soon learned that intensive exploration with efforts to review the emotional life of the patient, especially his sexual adjustment, were likely to be followed by deterioration of his behavior on the ward and a type of fantasy usually encountered only in psychoses. The disorders of behavior and experience were not characteristic of delirium or confusional states, which might have been secondary to the infectious process. They instead took the form of a paranoid panic with ideas of persecution or of euphoric overactivity with aggressive primitive behavior, such as defecation on the floor. The most common picture was one similar to those encountered in severe morbid grief reactions, with a sense of emptiness, excessive hostility to any newcomer, agitation, and a feeling of loss of identity similar to that seen in states of depersonalization.

In patients whom we came to know well, we encountered striking fantasies referring to an awareness of having the deceased person incorporated into the abdomen and actually having to be expelled or thrown up by the patient. There was a remarkable confusion about the functions of the various body organs—the colon being described, for instance, as the esophagus or the lining of the body appearing as though it were open to the entrance or departure of another human being, not only the dead person but also living individuals who were hated by the patient. The awareness of something alive in the abdomen was described with a conviction and emotional reality similar to those found in the somatic delusions of patients with involutional melancholia.

CONCLUSION

Consideration of the relationship of life situation, emotional states, and colon function in a disease such as ulcerative colitis will profitably include the total mental status and the overall disease picture, rather than being restricted to the local relationship of colon function and concurrent alleged emotional state. A common life situation preceding the onset of ulcerative colitis is the loss of a key person in the human environment on whom the patient has been dependent for interaction and emotional security. The mental status seen during acute phases of this disease is often that of a morbid grief reaction in which adequate mourning is replaced by an impaired mental state combined with a visceral disorder. Fantasies of having incorporated the dead person as though this were a concrete physical event after the pattern experienced by patients with involutional melancholia may be features of the psychiatric disorder. Control of the life situation by manipulating the human orbit may be a rewarding form of psychiatric management.

The person lost may be replaced temporarily by the therapist or by a suitable person under his direction. Such substitution, or role-taking therapy, is most useful during the acute emergencies of a severe episode and must be followed by the establishment of more protracted legitimate forms of dependent interaction. Efforts at intensive exploration run the risk of being followed by psychotic-like episodes or primitive behavior and by intensification of somatic delusions or paranoid manifestations.

Spontaneous changes in the life situation could be observed to take place concurrent with fluctuations in the disease picture. In addition to loss by death, such changes included loss by disillusionment or rejection, and the temporary inaccessability of an obligatory partner through the latter's illness, mental disease, or intense preoccupation with an emotional problem.

REFERENCES

Daniels, H.E. (1942). Psychiatric aspects of ulcerative colitis. *New England Journal of Medicine* 226:178-184.

Groen, J. (1947). Psychogenesis and psychotherapy of ulcerative colitis. *Psychosomatic Medicine* 9:151-174.

Lindemann, Erich (1944). Symptomatology and management of acute grief. *American Journal of Psychiatry* 101:141-148.

———(1945). Psychiatric aspects of the conservative treatment of ulcerative colitis. *Archives of Neurology and Psychiatry* 53:322-325.

Murray, C.D. (1930). Psychogenic factors in the etiology of ulcerative colitis and bloody diarrhea. *American Journal of Medical Science* 180:239-248.

Neuropsychiatric Observations After the Coconut Grove Fire

By Stanley Cobb, M.D., and Erich Lindemann, M.D.

The Coconut Grove fire was a tragedy never to be forgotten in New England history. It took place in the evening following the Harvard-Yale football game, in a Boston nightclub where couples and families had gathered to celebrate the occasion. Four hundred and ninety-one persons lost their lives; thirty-nine living casualties were brought to the Massachusetts General Hopsital and segregated on a ward where they received the most recently approved burn treatment. Ida M. Cannon, the head social worker, wrote of their predicament, "Under the urgency of a disaster such as this the focus of clinical concern of the physician and nurse is sharpened, the area of attention markedly restricted. At the same time the personal and social aspects of the patients' problems are especially acute and distressing. For them the experience of sudden shift from well-

being and gaiety to painful and serious injury, and for many
the death of some loved ones, created deeply disturbing com-
plications that needed special psychiatric attention. Deep grief
experience came to many patients at a time when they were
enduring physical suffering and, immobilized and isolated,
they could not act for themselves. The necessary "no visitors"
precaution made it more difficult to turn to their families for
help.[1]

Chapter 3 presents a condensed version of Dr. Lindemann's
experiences with the fire victims.[2] *His emphasis on making a*
graphic record of their interactions can be seen as a carry-over
from his drug research period, whereas his concern for what
happens to these patients when they leave the hospital fore-
shadows his future interest in community mental health.

This report deals with the problems involved in the emotional adjustment of the patient to the Coconut Grove disaster,
with all its implications—disfigurement, lasting disability,
loss of work, bereavement, and disturbed social situations. We
wanted to learn how to recognize those patients who are liable
to emotional disorders, to prevent such disorders if possible,
and to help those who had become victims of untoward emotional reactions.

The first request for psychiatric help came through the social
workers who were serving as liaison personnel with relatives
and friends. They soon had become aware of the fact that the
emotional upset following the discovery of a body had attained, in some of the relatives, the proportions of a major
psychiatric condition and needed trained intervention. It was
at their insistence that we first witnessed states of acute grief.

[1]Dr. Lindemann's original report, containing fuller case histories, was edited by Dr. Cobb
for inclusion in the cited volume. It has again been somewhat condensed for inclusion here.
[2]*Management of the Coconut Grove Burns at the Massachusetts General Hospital*, J.B.
Lippincott, Phila., 1943, pp. 12-13.

From observing extreme reactions in the relatives, we concluded that similar reactions might occur in the patients on the ward as soon as they were recovered enough to deal with the disruption of their social relationships. On the eighth day after the disaster, the psychiatrists were invited to review all patients still on the ward. The occasion was a dramatic psychotic episode in a woman who had not been confused and was not then showing signs of impairment of brain functions but who had responded to the news of the death of her husband and son with a state of excitement and intense paranoid suspicions about the ward personnel. She believed that nurses and doctors were considering her an immoral, sinful person and were plotting to detain her and to prepare for her punishment. She insisted on leaving against the advice of the physicians and was able to persuade members of her family to demand her release. Psychiatric inquiry showed that this patient had had a former episode of mental abnormality with obsessive fears, depression, and mild agitation. Follow-up reports show that her subsequent adjustment has remained quite precarious, with spurts of overactivity alternating with periods of apathy but that she has not developed any frank psychosis.

In the light of this incident it was decided to make a brief psychiatric study of all the patients left on the ward in order to be able to anticipate subsequent emotional disturbances. Seventeen patients have been so reviewed. Each received a neurologic and psychiatric examination. Abnormalities in mental status were recorded. A psychiatric history was obtained from the patient, and, with the help of social workers, from the relatives. Plans then were made with surgeons, social workers, and the occupational therapy workers for the best care of each patient in the light of our observations about his emotional reaction patterns and his former modes of adjustment.

The group as a whole was of fair intellectual level. Except in one case there was no aphasia or apraxia, and the disturbances of memory were limited to amnestic scotomata, which it was difficult to separate from the effects of impairment of consciousness at the time of the accident.

One patient showed a clear-cut picture of cerebral lesion. Two patients developed frank psychotic episodes and in both instances the former history showed clear-cut indication of previous maladjustment. A history of a frank neurosis in the past was present in two patients. They did not show any signs of mental derangement during the hospital stay and did not become serious nursing problems. Their difficulties became most conspicuous after discharge from the hospital. The return to normal life activities was slow, and previous psychoneurotic manifestations recurred in exaggerated form, requiring systematic psychiatric therapy.

The other patients did not show any significant history of previous psychiatric difficulties. None of them had positive symptoms of neurosis, psychosis, or personality defect.

Seven patients became problems of psychiatric study and management because their recovery was complicated by severe grief. This study provided an unusual opportunity to observe the mechanisms of grief by which the bereaved person reestablished his equilibrium after the loss of a beloved. Within a few days after the incident, as soon as the patient recovered from the shock and clouded consciousness, the question arose of when to tell him about his loss. It was obvious that both the physical and mental condition must be such that the individual could tolerate the message.

Our observations, then, concern seven bereaved patients. Three of them said that they had been told just at the right time. Three felt that they had been reasonably certain of the loss, and the final confirmation appeared as a relief of uncertainty rather than as an additional shock. Frequent discussions between the surgeon and the psychiatrist were necessary to weigh somatic and psychologic factors bearing on the right moment of delivering the message of bereavement.

One patient suspended all inquiry about the details of her husband's fate for more than four weeks, deliberately occupying her thoughts with personal friends and pleasant fantasies and recollections. When, however, her relatives visited her, they became more and more uneasy because the range of topics discussed in conversation was necessarily small. Any reference to the lost person and any attempt at planning the future had to be avoided. It finally became the psychiatrist's task to confront the patient with the sad news. This was done in the slow process of gradually recalling to her the details of her family life and her relationships to her children and relatives and making it inescapable for her to inquire positively about the fate of her husband. Her first reaction was to blame her relatives for withholding the news, and in the subsequent interviews there was a marked hostility against the psychiatrist. After a grief period of less than a week she continued to make an unperturbed recovery so far as her physical condition was concerned. She has refused any further relationship with the psychiatrist but has apparently made a fairly good adjustment at home.

The second task of the psychiatrist was to assist the person with the adjustment to the loss and to steer him through the disturbing period of intense emotional upheaval which ensued during the subsequent weeks. It became apparent that the patients showed considerable variation in their reactions. Common to all of them, however, was the syndrome described in chapter 4.

It seems that the grieving person can delay his grieving period but not avoid it, and individuals who show no signs of grief during the period of convalescence from their somatic injuries are likely to have disabling disturbances at a later period. Prophylactic care is most important here. The patient must be allowed to carry through his grief reaction at the optimal time without undue delay; he must be assisted in his efforts to extricate himself from the bondage to the deceased, to be prepared to face the task of social readjustment when he leaves the hospital.

In addition to these problems of clinical management, the solution of certain research problems has been brought nearer realization through the cooperation of a group of patients. For some time, the Psychiatric Service of Massachusetts General Hospital has been interested in the physiologic and psychologic aspects of acute grief. Since acute grief is one of the most frequent psychogenic factors found in patients with psychosomatic disorders, such as asthma, colitis, and rheumatoid arthritis, we have been anxious to discover what physiologic features of grief might play a role in contributing to the etiology of these disorders.

In the Coconut Grove fire victims there was evidence of disturbances in autonomic functions. The pupils were generally large. During the surges of acute grief described above, there was usually sighing respiration, "hot waves" to the head, flushed face, and perspiration. Systematic spirograms were not satisfactory because of the chest involvement. We have, however, been able to carry on observations in bereaved relatives who showed the same sighing respiration. There is indication that the altered respiratory activity, combined with the disturbance of sleep and appetite, may be the nucleus of a physiologic disturbance that forms the background for the "emotional distress" described by the patients.

Our data are somewhat more complete for the study of the amount of activity presented by the fire victims and bereaved patients. It is known that in states of morbid depression a patient is likely to be retarded in speech and action. Contrary to expectation, in the state of depression and unhappiness following such a disaster experience, there is not a reduction in activity as is seen in cases of psychotic depression; instead, there is an increase in need for activity.

This need for activity can be strikingly demonstrated by a new measuring device, the "interaction chronogram" (Chapple and Lindemann 1942). This consists of a tape that moves at the speed of five inches per minute. An observer behind a one-way screen presses a separate key for each of the two participants in an interview to record verbal and gestural activity. Graphs made in this way during a psychiatric interview show both the patient's and the psychiatrist's balance of activity and inactivity at any given time. They furnish an objective record of the patient's capacity to be active, of his hesitations after questions, and of his tendency to "out-talk" the examiner in conversation. We found that all bereaved persons examined showed a positive slope of the action-silence curve, indicating a surplus of activity over inactivity. Figures 1-6 present interaction chronograms that show the striking differences in activity rates observed in patients with acute grief and in those suffering from other forms of morbid depression.

Figures 1 and 2 represent mood disturbances that were seen in the Psychiatric Service. They showed depressive reactions with the usual slowness of response and underactivity. Figure 3 shows a patient who was found in a mild manic state of overactivity with euphoria and cheerful thought-content. Contrary to expectations, the interaction chronograms of bereaved patients, as shown in Figures 4, 5, and 6 show overactivity and no retardation and slowness of response seen in other depressed states.

This finding is of special significance because it indicates a drive for activity in individuals who at the same time complain about apathy, inability to initiate any action, and lack of interest in their ordinary pursuits. Our observations seem to indicate that there is a good deal of drive for activity and the lack of "conduct patterns" by which to express their drive. A good many daily activities were conditioned to the presence of the deceased and could no longer operate. But more than that, other activities not obviously connected with the presence of

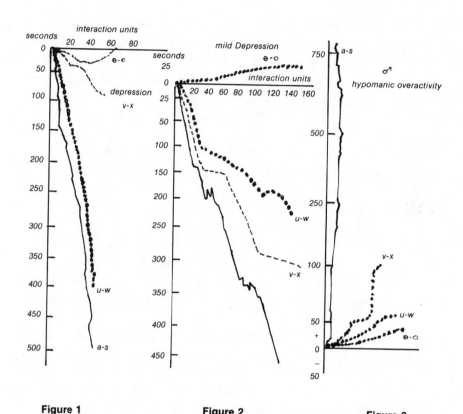

Figure 1   **Figure 2**   **Figure 3**

Fig. 1. A morbid depression of mood not complicated by grief. Note the steep negative slope of the A-S curve & the U-W curve. The deficit of action in relationship to silence on the part of the patient is 480 seconds in a 40-minute interview. **Fig. 2.** A milder depression. The steep negative slope of the A-S curve is interrrupted by occasional periods of increased activity but there is still a marked deficit in action. **Fig. 3.** A patient in a mild manic episode with marked overactivity. The surplus of activity over silence in a 40-minute interview is 750 seconds.

In the above figures **1-6** , A minus S represents the relationship of the patient's periods of activity to his periods of silence, in a cumulative series; U minus W represents the relationship of the patient's double actions (such as his interruptions

the deceased have lost their meaning and are carried out only with difficulty. It is, therefore, not surprising that only two of our series of mourning individuals were able to resume their

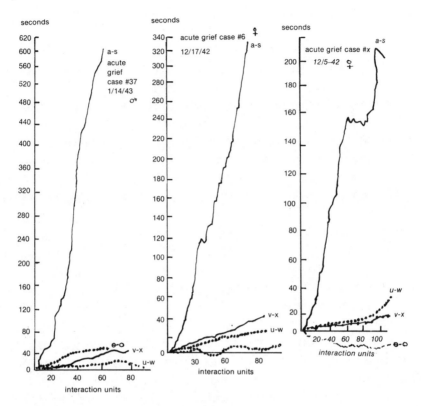

Figure 4 **Figure 5** **Figure 6**

Fig. 4. Acute grief reaction. The patient appears depressed during the interview but shows considerable overactivity. The A-S curve has a steep positive slope. The surplus of action over silence in a 40-minute interview is 610 seconds. **Fig. 5.** Acute grief reaction with strongly depressive thought content. Note the markedly positive slope of the A-S curve. The curve resembles that of Fig. 3. There is a marked surplus of activity over silence. **Fig. 6.** Acute grief reaction with less pronounced overactivity.

of the doctor) to his failure to respond; V minus X represents the relationship of the doctor's double actions to his failure to respond; and E minus O represents the relationship of the patient's initiations to those of the doctor.

ordinary activities after leaving the hospital. The others still find themselves aimless, lacking in initiative, and looking to others for suggestions to follow.

DISCUSSION

Of the thirty-nine patients admitted to the hospital, seven died within sixty-two hours. Of the survivors, at least fourteen presented neuropsychiatric problems. This high incidence may seem surprising, but it fits well with the experiences of psychiatrists working in general hospitals. Forty-five to fifty-five percent of the patient population are likely to present psychologic factors in their problems.

Conditions predominantly attributable to cerebral damage were rare, probably because they usually lead to death. Conditions predominantly the result of psychogenic factors showed a high incidence. In all patients with clear-cut neuroses and psychoses, the psychiatric history offered clues as to the likelihood of such development under stress. This observation fits well with recent studies concerning traumatic neuroses in the armed forces (Ross 1941, Gillespie 1942). It seems well-founded that induction boards refuse admission to the armed forces to candidates who show a former history of psychosis or psychoneurosis.

The more severe emotional disturbances encountered in formerly well-adjusted patients seemed to be attributable not so much to the impersonal effects of the disaster (fright and horror) as to the problems in personal and social relationships involving conflict and guilt. Similar observations were reported by Sargant and Slater (1940) and Wilson (1941), after the disaster experiences of members of the British armed forces and civilian population.

Psychiatric assistance in the solution of these personal problems and in readjustment after a social crisis forms an important part of the care of disaster victims. Unless the psychiatrist has an opportunity to see all the victims of a disaster, danger signals and opportunities for help along psychologic lines may be overlooked, since they are by no means obvious to the untrained worker.

Our observations seem to indicate that the psychiatrist can operate as a useful member of a disaster unit. His work may be divided into three phases:

Phase 1. In the first few days severe shock and lifesaving procedures occupy the field. Apathy, excitement, confusion, and delirious states must be handled by proper sedation and proper surroundings. In our present observations, we have only indirect evidence of the victim's emotional states at that time. Two patients complained of the lack of a chance for enduring contact with one person—doctor, attendant, or nurse: Everything seemed to change; every person who arrived seemed to be new; no information or outside news was available; and the days were ones of utter bewilderment, offering no frame of reference. It might be advisable to have the number of ward personnel as small as circumstances permit or so divided that patients have a chance to deal with the same person repeatedly.

Phase 2. The second phase deals with the psychiatric care of the convalescent patient, advising him in his transitory problems, determining when messages should be delivered or revelations made, and managing with the patient his efforts to readjust.

Phase 3. The third phase deals with the psychiatric care of the convalescent patient after he leaves the hospital and with his proper readjustment in the community. In this manner, we can have reasonable hope of preventing the occurrence of prolonged maladjustment or traumatic neurosis.

During the first phase, the psychiatrist's chief contribution is his aid to the relatives and his counsel to the medical social worker who is dealing with the numerous problems of family and work relationships. During the second phase, he is intimately involved with the internist and surgeon and must continue his contact with the social worker, which becomes even more important during the third phase, when social readjustment forms the center of interest. Throughout the three periods, not the least important of the psychiatrist's responsibilities is determining what can safely be delegated to the medical social worker and guiding her in her efforts.

It seems fair to conclude that it is desirable to make a psychiatric evaluation of patients early in the course of their hospital care. In addition, continued psychiatric attention should be available to those patients in a precarious emotional state. Finally, aid in readjustment should be provided after leaving the hospital, especially for cases of bereavement.

REFERENCES

Chapple, E.D., and Lindemann, E. (1942). Clinical implications of measurements of interaction rates in psychiatric interviews. *Applied Anthropology* 1:1-11.

Gillespie, R.D. (1942). *Psychological Effects of War on Citizen and Soldier.* New York: Norton.

Ross, T.A. (1941). *Lectures in War Neuroses.* Baltimore: Williams and Wilkins.

Sargant, W., and Slater, E. (1940). Acute war neuroses. *Lancet* 2:1.

Wilson, A.T.M. (1941). Reactive emotional disorders. *Practitioner* 146:254-258.

Chapter 4

Symptomatology and Management of Acute Grief

Many readers of this collection will already be familiar with this chapter, which consists of Lindemann's best-known paper on the subject of grief. It has been reprinted scores of times and is required reading for many students preparing for human services careers. It may acquire fresh meaning in the present context, where it can be understood as the climax of a search that led from the clues offered by postsurgical states through those evident in ulcerative colitis and finally to the unmistakable grief syndrome of the disaster victims.

The similarity between the behavior of the fire victims and that of the ulcerative colitis patients Lindemann described in an unpublished paper (1945) was striking: "It was obvious that in order to understand these ulcerative colitis patients it was necessary to study a large number of reactions in other people; and observations at the time of the Coconut Grove fire showed the characteristic results of losing a beloved person. To our surprise, we found that same poverty of effective modes of behavior in maintaining social relationships, the same need for

*activity, and the same tendency to deteriorate in behavior when
an intimate relationship is forced upon them."*

*To our surprise: it is always surprising when someone comes
along to look at an everyday phenomenon with fresh insight.*

At first glance, acute grief would not seem to be a medical or
psychiatric disorder in the strict sense of the word but rather a
normal reaction to a distressing situation. However, the understanding of reactions to traumatic experiences whether or not
they represent clear-cut neuroses has become of ever-increasing
importance to the psychiatrist. Bereavement or the sudden
cessation of social interaction seems to be of special interest
because it is often cited among the alleged psychogenic factors
in psychosomatic disorders. Furthermore, the enormous increase in grief reactions as a result of war casualties demands an
evaluation of their probable effect on the mental and physical
health of our population.

The points to be made in chapter 4 are as follows:

1. Acute grief is a definite syndrome with psychological and
   somatic symptomatology.
2. This syndrome may appear immediately after a crisis, or it
   may be delayed; it may be exaggerated or apparently
   absent.
3. In place of the typical syndrome, there may appear distorted pictures, each of which represents one special aspect of the grief syndrome.
4. By appropriate techniques these distorted pictures can be
   successfully transformed into a normal grief reaction with
   resolution.

Our observations were based on 101 patients. Included are (1)
psychoneurotic patients who lost a relative during the course of
treatment, (2) relatives of patients who died in the hospital, (3)

bereaved disaster victims (Coconut Grove Fire) and their close relatives, and (4) relatives of members of the armed forces. The investigations consisted of a series of psychiatric interviews. Both the timing and the content of the discussions were recorded. These records were subsequently analyzed in terms of the symptoms reported and of the changes in mental status observed progressively through a series of interviews. The psychiatrist avoided all suggestions and interpretations until the picture of symptomatology and spontaneous reaction tendencies of the patients had become clear from the records. The somatic complaints offered important leads for objective study.

SYMPTOMATOLOGY OF NORMAL GRIEF

The picture shown by persons in acute grief is remarkably uniform. Common to all was the following syndrome: sensations of somatic distress occurring in waves lasting from twenty minutes to an hour at a time, a feeling of tightness in the throat, choking with shortness of breath, need for sighing, an empty feeling in the abdomen, lack of muscular power, and an intense subjective distress described as tension or mental pain. The patient soon learns that these waves of discomfort can be precipitated by visits, by mentioning the deceased, and by receiving sympathy. There is a tendency to avoid the syndrome at any cost, to refuse visits lest they should precipitate the reaction, and to deliberately keep from thought all references to the deceased.

The striking features were the following: (1) The marked tendency to sighing respiration was most conspicuous when the patient was made to discuss his grief. (2) The complaint about lack of strength and exhaustion is universal and is described as follows: "It is almost impossible to climb up a stairway." "Everything I lift seems so heavy." "The slightest effort makes me feel exhausted." "I can't walk to the corner without feeling exhausted." (3) Digestive symptoms are described as follows: "The food tastes like sand." "I have no appetite at all." "I stuff the food down because I have to eat." "My saliva won't flow." "My abdomen feels hollow." "Everything seems slowed up in my stomach."

The sensorium is generally somewhat altered. There is commonly a slight sense of unreality and a feeling of increased emotional distance from other people (sometimes they appeared shadowy or small), and there is intense preoccupation with the image of the deceased. A patient who lost his daughter in the Coconut Grove disaster visualized his girl in the telephone booth calling for him and was much troubled by the loudness with which his name was called by her; he was so vividly preoccupied with the scene that he became oblivious of his surroundings. A young navy pilot lost a close friend; the friend remained a vivid part of the pilot's imagery, not in terms of a religious survival but in terms of an imaginary companion. He ate with him and talked over problems with him—for instance, discussing with him his plan of joining the Air Corps. Up to the time of the study, six months later, the young pilot denied the fact that the boy was no longer with him. Some patients are much concerned about this aspect of their grief reaction because they feel that it indicates approaching insanity.

Another strong preoccupation is with feelings of guilt. The bereaved searches the time before the death for evidence of failure to do right by the lost one. He accuses himself of negligence and exaggerates minor omissions. After the fire disaster, the central topic of discussion for a young married woman was the fact that her husband died after he left her following a quarrel; and for a young man whose wife died, that he fainted too soon to save her.

In addition, there is often disconcerting loss of warmth in relationship to other people, a tendency to respond with irritability and anger, and a wish not to be bothered by others at a time when friends and relatives make a special effort to keep up friendly relationships. These feelings of hostility, surprising and quite inexplicable to the patients, disturbed them and again were often taken as signs of approaching insanity. Great efforts are made to handle them, and the result is often a formalized, stiff manner of social interaction.

The activity throughout the day of the severely bereaved person shows remarkable changes. There is no retardation of action and speech; quite to the contrary there is a push of speech, especially when talking of the deceased. There is restlessness, inability to sit still, moving about in an aimless fashion, and a continual searching for something to do. There is, however, at the same time, a painful lack of capacity to initiate and maintain organized patterns of activity. What is done is done with lack of zest, as though one were going through the motions. The bereaved clings to the daily routine of prescribed activities; but these activities do not proceed in the automatic, self-sustaining fashion that characterizes normal work but have to be carried on with effort, as though each fragment of the activity becomes a special task. The bereaved is surprised to find how large a part of his customary activity was done in some meaningful relationship to the deceased and has now lost its significance. Especially the habits of social interaction—meeting friends, making conversation, and sharing enterprises with others—seem to have been lost. This loss leads to a strong dependency on anyone who will stimulate the bereaved to activity and serve as the initiating agent.

These five points—somatic distress, preoccupation with the image of the deceased, guilt, hostile reactions, and loss of patterns of conduct—seem to be pathognomonic for grief. There may be added a sixth characteristic, shown by patients who border on pathological reactions, which is not so conspicuous as the others but nevertheless often striking enough to color the whole picture: This is the appearance of traits of the deceased in the behavior of the bereaved, especially symptoms shown during the last illness, or behavior that may have been shown at the time of the tragedy. A bereaved person is observed or finds himself walking in the manner of his deceased father. He looks in the mirror and believes that his face appears just like that of the deceased. He may show a change of interests in the direction of the former activities of the deceased and may start enterprises entirely different from his former pursuits. A wife who lost her husband, an insurance agent, found herself writing to many insurance companies offering her services with somewhat exaggerated schemes. It symmed a regular observation in these patients that the painful preoccupation with the image of the deceased described above was transformed into preoccupation with symptoms or personality traits of the lost person, but now displaced to their own bodies and activities by identification.

COURSES OF NORMAL GRIEF REACTIONS

The duration of a grief reaction seems to depend on the success with which a person does the grief work—namely, emancipation from the bondage to the deceased, readjustment to the environment in which the deceased is missing, and the formation of new relationships. One of the big obstacles to this work seems to be the fact that many patients try to avoid the intense distress connected with the grief experience and to avoid the expression of emotion necessary for it. The male victims after the Coconut Grove fire appeared in the early psychiatric interviews to be in a state of tension with tightened facial musculature, unable to relax for fear that they might "break down." It required considerable persuasion to yield to the grief process before they were willing to accept the discomfort of bereavement. One assumed a hostile attitude toward the psychiatrist, refusing to allow any references to the deceased and rather rudely asking him to leave. This attitude remained throughout his stay on the ward, and the prognosis for his condition is not good in the light of other observations. Hostility of this sort was encountered on only occasional visits with the other patients. They became willing to accept the grief process and to embark on a program of dealing in memory with the deceased person. As soon as this became possible there seemed to be a rapid relief of tension and the subsequent interviews were rather animated conversations in which the deceased was idealized and in which misgivings about the future adjustment were worked through.

Examples of the psychiatrist's role in assisting patients in their readjustment after bereavement are contained in the following case histories. The first shows a very successful readjustment:

A woman, aged forty, lost her husband in the fire. She had a history of good adjustment previously. She had one child, who was ten years old. When she heard about her husband's death she was extremely depressed, cried bitterly, did not want to live, and for three days showed a state of utter dejection.

When seen by the psychiatrist, she was glad to have assistance and described her painful preoccupation with memories of her husband and her fear that she might lose her mind. She had a vivid visual image of his presence, picturing him as going to work in the morning and herself as wondering whether he would return in the evening and whether she could stand his not returning. She then described to herself how he does return, plays with the dog, and receives his child; and she gradually tried to accept the fact that he was not there any more. It was only after ten days that she succeeded in accepting his loss and then only after having described in detail the remarkable qualities of her husband, the tragedy of his having to stop his activities at the pinnacle of his success, and his deep devotion to her.

In the subsequent interviews, she explained with some distress that she had become very much attached to the examiner and that she waited for the hour of his coming. This reaction she considered disloyal to her husband but at the same time she could accept the fact that it was a hopeful sign of her ability to fill the gap he had left in her life. She then showed a marked drive for activity, making plans for supporting herself and her little girl, mapping out the preliminary steps for resuming her old profession as secretary, and making efforts to secure help from the occupational therapy department in reviewing her knowledge of French. Her convalescence, both emotional and somatic, progressed smoothly, and she made a good adjustment immediately on her return home.

A man of fifty-two, successful in business, lost his wife with whom he had lived in happy marriage. The information given him about his wife's death confirmed his suspicion of several days. He responded with a severe grief reaction, with which he was unable to cope. He did not want to see visitors, was ashamed of breaking down, and asked to be permitted to stay in the hospital on the psychiatric service, when his physical condition would have permitted his discharge, because he wanted further assistance. Any mention of his wife produced a severe wave of depressive reaction, but with psychiatric assistance he gradually became willing to go through this painful process. After three days on the psychiatric service he seemed well enough to go home.

He showed a high rate of verbal activity, was restless, needed to be occupied continually, and felt that the experience had whipped him into a state of restless overactivity. As soon as he returned home he took an active part in his business, assuming a post in which he had a great many telephone calls. He also took over the role of amateur psychiatrist to another bereaved person, spending time with him and comforting him for his loss. In his eagerness to start anew, he developed a plan to sell all his former holdings, including his house and his furniture, and to give away anything that could remind him of his wife. Only after considerable discussion was he able to see that this would mean avoiding immediate grief at the price of an act of poor judgment. Again, he had to be encouraged to deal with his grief reactions in a more direct manner. He made a good adjustment.

With eight to ten interviews in which the psychiatrist shares the grief work, and with a period of from four to six weeks, it was ordinarily possible to settle an uncomplicated and undistorted grief reaction. This was the case in all but one of the thirteen Coconut Grove fire victims.

MORBID GRIEF REACTIONS

Morbid grief reactions represent distortions of normal grief. The conditions mentioned here were transformed into "normal reactions" and then found their resolution.

Delay of Reaction. The most striking and most frequent reaction of this sort is delay or postponement. If the bereavement occurs at a time when the patient is confronted with important tasks and when there is necessity for maintaining the morale of others, he may show little or no reaction for weeks or even much longer. A brief delay is described in the following example.

A girl of seventeen lost both parents and her boyfriend in the fire and was herself severely burned, with marked involvement of the lungs. Throughout her stay in the hospital, her attitude was that of cheerful acceptance without any sign of adequate distress. When she was discharged at the end of three weeks, she appeared cheerful, talked rapidly with a considerable flow of ideas, and seemed eager to return home and to assume the role of parent for her two younger siblings. Except for slight feelings of "lonesomeness" she complained of no distress.

This period of griefless acceptance continued for the next two months, even when the household was dispersed and her younger siblings were placed in other homes. Not until the end of the tenth week did she begin to show a true state of grief with marked feelings of depression, intestinal emptiness, tightness in her throat, frequent crying, and vivid preoccupation with her deceased parents.

That a delay in reaction may involve years became obvious first by the fact that patients in acute bereavement about a recent death may soon be found preoccupied with grief about a person who died many years earlier. For example, a woman of thirty-eight, whose mother had died recently and who had responded to her mother's death with a surprisingly severe reaction, was found to be but mildly concerned with her mother's death but deeply engrossed with unhappy and perplexing fantasies concerning the death of her brother, who died twenty years before under dramatic circumstances from metastasizing carcinoma after amputation of his arm had been postponed too long. The discovery that a former unresolved grief reaction may be precipitated in the course of the discussion of another recent event was soon demonstrated in psychiatric interviews by patients who showed all the traits of a true grief reaction when the topic of a former loss arose.

The precipitating factor for the delayed reaction may be a deliberate recall of circumstances surrounding the death or a spontaneous occurrence in the patient's life. A peculiar form of this is the circumstance that a patient develops the grief reaction at the time when he himself is as old as the person who died. For instance, a railroad worker, aged forty-two, appeared in the psychiatric clinic with a picture that was undoubtedly a grief reaction for which he had no explanation. It turned out that when he was twenty-two years old, his mother, then forty-two, had committed suicide.

Distorted Reactions. The delayed reactions may occur after an interval not marked by any abnormal behavior or distress but in which there developed an alteration in the patient's conduct perhaps not conspicuous or serious enough to lead him to a psychiatrist. These alterations may be considered the surface manifestations of an unresolved grief reaction, which may respond to fairly simple and quick psychiatric management if recognized. They can be classified as follows:

1. There may be overactivity without a sense of loss. There may instead be a sense of well-being and zest, the activities being of an expansive and adventurous nature and bearing semblance to the activities formerly carried out by the deceased, as described previously.

2. Symptoms belonging to the last illness of the deceased may be acquired. This type of patient appears in medical clinics and is often labeled as suffering from hypochondriasis or hysteria. To what extent actual alterations of physiological functions occur under these circumstances will have to be a field of further careful inquiry. I owe to Dr. Chester Jones a report about a patient whose electrocardiogram showed a definite change during a period of three weeks, which began two weeks after her father died of heart disease.

3. Although this sort of symptom formation "by identification" may still be considered conversion symptoms such as we know from hysteria, there is another type of disorder doubtlessly presenting a recognized medical disease—namely, a group of psychosomatic conditions, predominantly ulcerative colitis, rheumatoid arthritis, and asthma. Extensive studies in ulcerative colitis have produced the following evidence: Thirty-three out of forty-one patients with ulcerative colitis developed their disease in close time relationship to the loss of an important person. Indeed, it was this observation that first gave the impetus for the present detailed study of grief. Two of the patients developed bloody diarrhea at funerals. In the others, it

developed within a few weeks after the loss. The course of the ulcerative colitis was strikingly benefited when this grief reaction was resolved by psychiatric technique.

4. At the level of social adjustment there often occurs a conspicuous alteration in the relationships with friends and relatives. The patient feels irritable, does not want to be bothered, avoids former social activities, and is afraid he might antagonize his friends by his lack of interest and his critical attitudes. Progressive social isolation follows, and the patient needs considerable encouragement in reestablishing his social relationships.

5. Whereas overflowing hostility appears spread out over all relationships, it may also occur as furious hostility against specific persons; the doctor or the surgeon may be bitterly accused for neglect of duty and the patient may assume that foul play has led to the death. It is characteristic that although patients talk a good deal about their suspicions and their bitter feelings, they are not likely to take any action against the accused, as a truly paranoid person might do.

6. Many bereaved persons struggled with much effort against feelings of hostility, which, to them, seem absurd, represent a vicious change in their characters, and should be hidden as much as possible. Some patients succeed in hiding their hostility but become wooden and formal, with affectivity and conduct resembling schizophrenic pictures. A typical report is this, "I go through all the motions of living. I look after my children. I do my errands. I go to social functions, but it is like being in a play; it doesn't really concern me. I can't have any warm feelings. If I were to have any feelings at all I would be angry with everybody." This patient's reaction to therapy was characterized by growing hostility against the therapist, and it required considerable skill to make her continue interviews in spite of the disconcerting hostility that she had been fighting so much. The absence of emotional display in this patient's face

and actions was quite striking. Her face had a masklike appearance, and her movements were formal, stilted, and robotlike, without the fine play of emotional expression.

7. Closely related to this picture is a lasting loss of patterns of social interaction. The patient cannot initiate any activity and is full of eagerness to be active; he is restless, cannot sleep, but throughout the day he will not start any activity unless "primed" by somebody else. He will be grateful at sharing activities with others but will not be able to make up his mind to do anything alone. The picture is one of lack of decision and initiative. Organized activities along social lines occur only if a friend takes the patient along and shares the activity with him. Nothing seems to promise reward; only the ordinary activities of the day are carried on, and these in a routine manner— falling apart into small steps, each of which has to be carried out with much effort and without zest.

8. There is, in addition, a picture in which a patient is active but in which most of his activities attain a coloring detrimental to his own social and economic existence. Such patients, with uncalled-for generosity, give away their belongings, are easily lured into foolish economic dealings, lose their friends and professional standing by a series of "stupid acts," and find themselves finally without family, friends, social status, or money. This protracted self-punitive behavior seems to occur without any awareness of excessive feelings of guilt. It is a particularly distressing grief picture because it is likely to hurt other members of the family and drag down friends and business associates.

9. This leads finally to the picture in which the grief reaction takes the form of a straight, agitated depression with tensions, agitation, insomnia, feelings of worthlessness, bitter self-accusation, and obvious need for punishment. Such patients may be dangerously suicidal.

A young man, aged thirty-two, had received only minor

burns and left the hospital apparently well on the road to recovery just before the psychiatric survey of the disaster victims took place. On the fifth day, he learned that his wife had died. He seemed somewhat relieved of his worry about her fate; he impressed the surgeon as being unusually well controlled during the short period he stayed in the hospital following his discovery of his wife's death.

On January 1, he was returned to the hospital by his family. Shortly after his return home he had become restless, did not want to stay at home, had taken a trip to relatives trying to find rest, had not succeeded, and had returned home in a state of marked agitation, appearing preoccupied, frightened, and unable to concentrate on any organized activity. His mental status presented a somewhat unusual picture: He was restless, could not sit still, and was unable to participate in any activity on the ward. He would try to read and would drop it after a few minutes, or he would try to play pingpong but would give it up after a short time. He would try to start conversations, break them off abruptly, and then fall into repeated murmured utterances, "Nobody can help me. When is it going to happen? I am doomed, am I not?"

With great effort it was possible to establish enough rapport to carry on interviews. He complained about his feeling of extreme tension, inability to breathe, generalized weakness and exhaustion, and his frantic fear that something terrible was going to happen, "I'm destined to live in insanity or I must die. I know that it is God's will. I have this awful feeling of guilt." With intense morbid guilt feelings, he reviewed incessantly the events of the fire. His wife had stayed behind. When he tried to pull her out, he had fainted and was shoved out by the crowd. She was burned while he was saved. "I should have saved her or I should have died too." He complained about being filled with an incredible violence and did not know what to do about it.

The rapport established with him lasted for only brief periods of time. He then would fall back into his state of intense agitation and muttering. He slept poorly even with large sedation. In the course of four days, he became somewhat more composed, had longer periods of contact with the psychiatrist, and seemed to feel that he was being understood and might be able to cope with his morbid feelings of guilt and violent impulses. However, on the sixth day of his hospital stay, after skillfully distracting the attention of his special nurse, he jumped through a closed window to a violent death.

If the patient is not conspicuously suicidal, it may nevertheless be true that he has a strong desire for painful experiences. Such patients are likely to desire shock treatment of some sort, which they picture as a cruel experience—such as electrocution might be.

A twenty-eight-year-old woman, whose twenty-month-old son was accidentally smothered, developed a state of severe agitated depression with self-accusations, inability to enjoy anything, hopelessness about the future, overflow of hostility against the husband and his parents; and excessive hostility against the psychiatrist. She insisted on electric-shock treatment and was finally referred to another physician who treated her. She responded to the shock treatments very well and felt relieved of her sense of guilt.

It is remarkable that agitated depressions of this sort represent only a small fraction of the pictures of grief in our series.

PROGNOSTIC EVALUATION

Our observations indicate that to a certain extent the type and severity of the grief reaction can be predicted. Patients with obsessive personality makeup and with a history of former depressions are likely to develop an agitated depression. Severe reactions seem to occur in mothers who have lost young children. The intensity of interaction with the deceased before his death appears significant. It is important to realize that such interaction does not have to be of the affectionate type; on the contrary, the death of a person who invited much hostility that could not well be expressed because of his status and claim to loyalty may be followed by a severe grief reaction in which hostile impulses are the most conspicuous feature. Not infrequently, the person who passed away represented a key person in a social system, his death being followed by disintegration of this social system and by a profound alteration of the living and social conditions for the bereaved. In such cases, readjustment presents a severe task quite apart from the reaction to the loss incurred. All these factors seem to be more important than a tendency in previous life to react with neurotic symptoms. In this way the most conspicuous forms of morbid identification were found in persons who had no former history of a tendency toward psychoneurotic reactions.

MANAGEMENT

Proper psychiatric management of grief reactions may prevent prolonged and serious alterations in the patient's social adjustment, as well as potential medical disease. The essential task facing the psychiatrist is that of sharing the patient's work—namely, his efforts at extricating himself from the bondage to the deceased and at finding new patterns of rewarding interaction. It is of the greatest importance to notice that not only overreaction but underreaction of the bereaved must be given attention. Delayed responses may occur at unpredictable moments, and the dangerous distortions of the grief reaction, not conspicuous at first, may be quite destructive later; such distortions may be prevented.

Religious agencies have led in dealing with the bereaved. They have provided comfort by giving the backing of dogma to the patient's wish for continued interaction with the deceased, have developed rituals that maintain the patient's interaction with others, and have counteracted the morbid guilt feelings of the patient by Divine Grace and by promising an opportunity for "making up" to the deceased at the time of a later reunion. Although these measures have helped countless mourners, comfort alone does not provide adequate assistance in the patient's grief work. He has to accept the pain of the bereavement. He has to review his relationships with the deceased, and he has to become acquainted with the alterations in his own modes of emotional reaction. His fear of insanity and his fear of accepting the surprising changes in his feelings, especially the overflow of hostility, must be worked through. He will have to express his sorrow and sense of loss. He will have to find an acceptable formulation of his future relationship to the deceased. He will have to verbalize his feelings of guilt, and he will have to find persons around him whom he can use as "primers" for the acquisition of new patterns of conduct. All this can be done in eight to ten interviews.

Special techniques are needed if hostility is the most marked feature of the grief reaction. The hostility may be directed against the psychiatrist, and the patient will have such guilt over his hostility that he will avoid further interviews. The help of a social worker or a minister or if these are not available, a member of the family, to urge the patient to continue coming to see the psychiatrist may be indispensable. If the tension and the depressive features are too great, a combination of benzedrine sulphate, five to ten mg twice a day, and sodium amytal, three grains before retiring, may be useful in first reducing emotional distress to a tolerable degree. Severe agitated depressive reactions may defy all efforts at psychotherapy and may respond well to shock treatment.

Since it is obvious that not all bereaved persons, especially those suffering because of war casualties, can have the benefit of expert psychiatric help, much of this knowledge will have to be passed on to auxiliary workers. Social workers and ministers will have to be on the lookout for the more ominous pictures, referring these to the psychiatrist while assisting the more normal reactions themselves.

ANTICIPATORY GRIEF REACTIONS

Although our studies were initially limited to reactions to actual death, it must be understood that grief reactions are just one form of separation reactions. Separation by death is characterized by its irreversibility and finality. Separation may, of course, occur for other reasons. We were at first surprised to find genuine grief reactions in patients who had not experienced a bereavement but who had experienced separation—for instance, with the departure of a member of the family into the armed forces. Separation in this case is not attributable to death but is under the threat of death. A common picture hitherto not appreciated is a syndrome that we have designated *anticipatory grief*. The patient is so concerned with her adjustment after the potential death of father or son that she goes through all the phases of grief and depression—heightened preoccupation with the departed, a review of all the forms of death that might befall him, and anticipation of the modes of readjustment that might be necessitated by it. Although this reaction may well form a safeguard against the impact of a sudden death notice, it can turn out to be a disadvantage at the occasion of reunion. For instance, a soldier just returned from the battlefront complained that his wife did not love him anymore and demanded immediate divorce. In such situations, the grief work had apparently been done so effectively that the patient had emancipated herself and the readjustment must now be directed toward new interaction. It is important to recognize this factor because many family disasters of this sort may be avoided through prophylactic measures.

REVIEW OF THE LITERATURE

Many of the observations contained in chapter 4 are, of course, not entirely new. Delayed reactions were described by Helene Deutsch (1937). Shock treatment in agitated depressions resulting from bereavement has recently been advocated by Myerson (1944). Morbid identification has been stressed at many points in the psychoanalytic literature and recently by Murray (1937). The relations of mourning and depressive psychoses have been discussed by Freud (1917), Melanie Klein (1940), and Abraham (1912). Wartime bereavement reactions were discussed by Wilson (1941). The reactions after the Coconut Grove fire were described in some detail in chapter 3. The effect of wartime separations was reported by Rosenbaum (1944). The incidence of grief reactions among the psychogenic factors in asthma and rheumatoid arthritis has been mentioned by Cobb, Bauer, and Whitney (1939) and by McDermott and Cobb (1939).

REFERENCES

Abraham, K. (1912). Notes on the psychoanalytic investigation and treatment of manic-depressive insanity and allied conditions. In *Selected Papers* London: Hogarth Press, 1927.

Cobb, S., Bauer, W., and Whitney, I. (1939). Environmental factors in rheumatoid arthritis. *Journal of the American Medical Association* 113:668-670.

Deutsch, H. (1937). Absence of grief. *Psychoanalytic Quarterly* 6:12-22.

Freud, S. (1917). Mourning and melancholia. *Standard Edition* 14:243-258.

Klein, M. (1940). Mourning and its relation to manic-depressive states. *International Journal of Psycho-Analysis* 21:125-153.

McDermott, N., and Cobb, S. (1939). Psychogenic factors in Asthma. *Psychosomatic Medicine* 1:204-341.

Murray, H.A. (1937). Visual manifestations of personality. *Journal of Abnormal and Social Psychology* 32:161-184.

Myerson, A. (1944). The use of shock therapy in prolonged grief reactions. *England Journal of Medicine* 230:9ff

Rosenbaum, M. (1944). Emotional aspects of wartime separations. *Family,* 24:337-341.

Wilson, A.T.M. (1941). Reactive emotional disorders. *Practitioner,* 146:254-258.

Individual Hostility and Group Integration

Like many other scientists of his generation, Lindemann was troubled by the problem of violence and how it could be transmitted by disturbed individuals—for example, Hitler—to groups and even to nations. In May 1948, the American Psychiatric Association, (APA) held a symposium on the origins of hostility, at which he gave the paper presented in chapter 5.

The fact that it was published, not in the APA journal, but in the relatively new journal of the Society for Applied Anthropology is significant, for Lindemann had recently acquired a set of nonmedical colleagues through his affiliation with the Department of Social Relations at Harvard. (In 1947, he accepted an invitation from Talcott Parsons and Clyde Kluckhohn to teach a course in clinical psychology in the new department.) He identified wholeheartedly with the effort to integrate concepts from anthropology, sociology, and social psychology and hoped that "the field of basic social sciences which is just emerging" would become "a bona fide subject for discussion in the medical school . . . namely: the study of interpersonal relationships of human beings."

The first part of chapter 5, a review of existing theories of aggression, represents the learner aspect of his new role as he joined the Department of Social Relations, whereas the second part contains the contribution he was able to make on the basis of firsthand clinical observations of hostile behavior.

Hostility between adult individuals and groups is of urgent concern not only to the psychiatrist but also to every citizen of the world today because of the rapidly expanding destructiveness of weapons of violence. In recent years, psychiatrists have become more and more conscious of the challenge before them to deal in a therapeutic manner with inclinations to violence of individuals as well as with those of nations and various groups within nations.

Unfortunately, the lag in social science compared to the physical and biological sciences is responsible for a gap in well-documented information concerning such everyday phenomena as the creation of hostile emotions and attitudes and their expression in hostile acts. This study can only try to clarify the concepts involved and point in the direction of a possible solution of the problems created by hostility. I shall confine myself to clinical observations with some reference to a few experiments in social psychology.

The term *hostility*, or *hostile impulses*, as used in psychiatry, is a more restricted concept than *aggression*. The latter refers to acts of mastery, determined manipulation, and executive behavior, which may often be quite free from the harmful or destructive quality inherent in hostility proper. One can distinguish the overt *hostile act* from *hostile emotion*, from more lasting *hostile sentiment*, and from *covert hostility*—the last inferred only from various apparently nonhostile fragments of behavior, which in their context, unknown to the actor, have a hostile effect often described as "unconscious hostile intent."

There immediately arises a basic question of the innate

versus the acquired nature of hostile impulses. Since Cannon's work (1915), we have been aware of the physiological processes involved in the emotions of rage and the attending hostile behavior in animals. No doubt there is a definitive physiological apparatus to make hostile action possible. Bard's work on sham rage (1934), which was later amplified by Rioch (1940), has given us some knowledge of the anatomical substratum requisite for the occurrence of the rage pattern upon perception of inimical stimuli. Man shares with certain carnivores the biological method of food acquisition that is predatory in relation to other animals; the capacity to hunt, hold, kill, and devour other living beings is inherent in our biological make-up. The problem of hostility does not arise in this area; only as other human beings or their property are involved as targets of violent destruction is this concept applicable.

Whether individuals are born to be more or less liable to hostile action is not answered by genetics. (For example, it is possible to breed more and less aggressive strains of mice. Allee [1938] studied these in relation to problems of dominance in animal societies.) Nobody seems to have identified genes relating to potential hostility in man.* However, differences in skeletomuscular form, as well as the reservoir and equipment for violent action, may well determine the social factors relating to the development of degrees of hostility. The small person who is resentful of his size, and the cripple restricted in freedom of mobility might be more hostile than the strong person whose strength secures him dominance and access to emotional rewards.

By far the more important sources of hostility are the learned responses engendered by the type of social interaction to which an individual has been exposed from the early days of his life

*The theory that males with an extra Y chromosome are more prone to violent behavior had not been put forward at the time this paper was written—E.B.L.

and from the type of group organization of which he is a part. The child who has learned to attain satisfaction of his needs without interfering with the need-satisfactions of others has had to abandon certain modes of behavior and replace them with others. At the same time, he has become aware that killing the enemy in wartime leads to a decoration for his father, that beating up the other fellow on the street gains him prestige among his comrades if not parental acclaim, and that his father's success in getting the better of a business competitor is a source of pride to the whole family. In other words, there is approved hostility and illegitimate hostility. It is more important to identify each group with its kind of hostility than it is to look for a moral code that applies to hostile acts in general.

It seems an old question to ask again for the primary source of hostility in human interaction. The appealing answer, documented well by Dollard et al. (1939), is that frustration—that is, interference with goal-directed action—will arouse hostile impulses; that the more severe the interference, the more severe the hostility; and that situations of challenge or loss that involve a frustration are often followed by a sequence of hostile impulses and actions. The frustration theory of hostility has been widely accepted. Rosenzweig (1944) traced the consequences of frustration in terms of extrapunitive and intrapunitive hostile behavior, and the psychoanalytic literature is full of examples of the variety of ways in which the hostile response, begotten by frustration or deprivation, may be inhibited, delayed, or replaced by apparently nonhostile reactions; or disappear altogether; or be reactivated by subsequent provocation.

In the last few years, increasing doubt has been cast on the all-exclusive role originally assigned to the frustration situation as the source of hostility. David Levy (1941) pointed out that not all frustration leads to hostility. Instead, it may lead to a modification or intensification of the goal-directed behavior. It seems that the problem is much more complex and that a great variety of factors are operating as potential sources for hostility. Consideration of such responses in terms of the individual only, without due regard to the structure of the human group in which they arise, is apt to oversimplify the answer to the problem.

The time characteristics of the frustrating situation should first be amplified. Security may be considered a state of affairs in which one does not anticipate any threat to the prevailing methods of securing rewards and need-satisfactions. Insecurity, then, is the awareness of a threat of *future* frustration. An important source of gratification for the individual is his status within a group; it determines the privilege of expecting certain actions from others in the group, as well as the obligation to fulfill certain of their expectations. Interference or threatened interference with group status may be brought about simply by altering the number of people in the group: The arrival or departure of one or more persons may serve as a source of hostility.

The term *hostile tension* has been used to indicate a state of readiness for hostile action in the face of such a threat, even though the target for action has not yet been found. Parsons (1947), taking threats to security as the starting point, reviewed some features of the social systems in which we and our patients live—all having in common the production of insecurity and ensuing hostile tension. The high rate of social mobility, the unstable family structure with rarely present father and reluctantly present mother, the lack of continuity in family and occupational life, and the exposure to conflicting claims and demands made possible by the overdevelopment of channels of communication all serve to reduce the likelihood of carrying on the present mode of adjustment with success into the foreseeable future. The forces demanding the transition from one frame of reference to the other become the object of hostile regard and are often personified to become suitable targets for hostile action. Even an individual who is not frustrated to any distressing degree may become a participant in hostile group sentiment in groups that find or consider themselves the victims of arbitrarily imposed changes. A person with a large reservoir of hostile tension will contribute to channeling and expressing the development of group sentiment into group action.

If insecurity widens the time pattern of frustration, a quantitative factor may be introduced by considering that an accumulation of minimal threats or provocations to angry responses may have the same effect of instigating hostile reactions as one powerful hostility-arousing event. This sort of provocation does not have to be a frustrating experience. A hostile action on the part of an individual or group may arouse counterhostility as the immediate response to the proper stimulus. The so-called rejecting mother or the group surrounding an individual with an inimical emotional climate may, by the omission of friendly acts just as by the commission of hostile deeds, create a growing reservoir of hostile tension requiring ever more primitive hostile acts for adequate discharge. Newcomb (1947) pointed out the vicious circle by which an individual or group once ready for hostile response gradually reduces the channels of communication with the potential enemy, thus preventing rectification of the early impressions of hostility and redress by friendly actions. Hostile isolation is likely to make hostile tension more enduring. The dammed-up hostility from other sources will then be channeled against the enemy, and any efforts to make the enemy unsuitable as a target will only arouse renewed and increased hostility. Every psychiatrist knows that the communication of hostile sentiments and their reappraisal in terms of the individuals or groups responsible for their creation is a crucial event in successful treatment; for he himself, in transference, temporarily becomes the target for hostile emotions.

The previous discussion by no means covers all possible sources, but it can at least form a basis for considering the fate of hostile impulses once they are aroused. Hostility, like other basic impulses, carries the demand for action—the removal or destruction of the stimulus. Should the stimulus agent disappear before he can become the object of hostile action, a hostile response still requires execution against substitute targets. The powerful self-punitive response seen in certain bereaved individuals after the death of a hated person suggests such a mechanism.

The most direct and primitive form of hostile action against an individual or group is killing and mutilation. There is also a wide gamut of other possible forms, ranging from primitive behavior to the many refined pursuits and tormentings of a victim that are still possible in our culture and even within the law—for example, malicious gossip or political blackmail. Nevertheless, there seems to be a great readiness for the hostile response to revert to the most primitive form when pressure of hostile tension reaches a certain maximum. The profusion of destructive fantasies in frustrated individuals, the furious self-destruction of melancholics, the arsenal of substitute reactions and more or less well-disguised defenses against hostility, and reaction-formations that have become common knowledge through psychoanalytic investigation need hardly be mentioned here.

When we examine the group relationships of the individual aroused to hostility, we see that anticipation of group punishment, or of self-punishment through uncomfortable guilt feelings vis-à-vis others, is likely to block the hostile act from execution or transform it into a relatively mild reaction. However, it is quite possible for an aroused individual to seek to make an alteration in his group's attitude toward his hostile acts by setting them in a more permissible or legitimate context. An observation made in our Psychiatric Service at the Massachusetts General Hospital serves as an illustration.

A twenty-two-year-old woman who had been the loser in a bitter rivalry with a more beautiful younger sister remained depressed for the first three weeks after her admission to the ward. She volunteered no conversation, answered questions as briefly as possible, ate little, and was unresponsive to attempts at arousing her interest. In psychotherapeutic interviews, no material was forthcoming.

At the end of this time, the other patients on the ward began to discuss the fact that the occupational therapist was leaving the Service. She was to be replaced by a young woman who was said to be very beautiful. The next day, the patient was seen to undergo a remarkable change in her rate of activity and her group participation. She became the center of a lively group in the ward, laughing and chatting gaily with the other patients and accepted by all as a friend. She began to eat well and showed no trace of depression. It was discovered that she had organized a bridge marathon that provided the ward population with employment and kept them highly involved, making it seem quite legitimate for them to refuse the new occupational therapist's invitations to participate in occupational therapy.

This new state of affairs lasted for three days. The entire ward was happy and free from many of the daily minor irritations which plague the interaction of nurses and patients. The only troubled person was the occupational therapist.

On the third day, however, the house officer, concerned about the occupational therapist's distress, prevailed on one of the women in the marathon to join the worker. Within a few hours, the whole new group enterprise had collapsed, and the patient returned to her previous isolation. That evening, she attempted suicide.

In this example, the patient's hostility had temporarily found a substitute target. It could be legitimately executed because it was disguised and made guilt-free through joint action in a group. Once this joint action stopped, the patient's hostility again had to be directed against herself.

This sort of observation is probably familiar to most psychiatrists in charge of therapeutic groups. But it deserves further systematic investigation. The control that determines license or inhibition for hostile action apparently remains flexible, varying with the group attitude. In turn, the hostility potential of a group may become channelized by the presence of a particularly hostile single member. Freud's analysis (1921) of the factors involved in lynching and mob violence and Redl's description (1942) of the behavior of adolescent boys who have formed groups or gangs with special codes of action, rigidly controlling the expression of hostility within the group and facilitating hostile attitudes and actions against out-groups, provide ample illustrations of this sort of individual and group interplay.

Parsons (1947) points out that as a nation grows the necessity of avoiding in-group tension is one of the sources of readiness to hate and to make a scapegoat of other national groups, adding to the danger of hostile action in the form of war. Nationalism, the fight for a religious tenet, and the struggle to maintain national superiority seem to be both broad and vague enough to permit channeling hostility in the direction of poorly defined and little investigated out-groups.

That the type of organization prevailing in a certain group may have great influence upon the hostility felt and displayed by its members, was shown in the well-known experiments of Lewin, Lippitt, and White (1939) in which groups of teenage boys differing in the type of leadership structure, some having centralized leadership (called autocratic), and some with group-determined action (called democratic), were compared for the amount of hostile expression and fighting recorded during certain standard observational periods. It turned out that members of the so-called autocratic group showed consid-

erably more overt hostility than those of the so-called democratic group and that the same boy would alter his level of
hostile expression according to the group of which he was a
member at a given time.

Of special interest for our consideration are situations in
which there is a sudden disturbance of group equilibrium.
Individuals who acquire an increment of hostile tension in
situations not suspected by them as being capable of so disturbing them—namely, in states of bereavement and the period
following major surgical operations—may show remarkable
changes in group interaction. We will not deal here with
whether or not the source of the hostility is primarily frustration involved in the loss of a beloved person or an organ of the
body. We are concerned rather with the disequilibrium of
group interaction observed to have occurred in the system of
human relations of such individuals.

A marked increment in hostile tension seems to be a common
consequence of surgery. It was directly expressed by one of our
women patients who, during a follow-up visit after an hysterectomy, knocked out her surgeon in a sudden display of
violence. The majority of such patients show varying degrees
of self-punitive preoccupation, lowered threshold for irrita-
tion, inclination to be more harsh than before with their
children and are generally more critical of those around them.
They exhibit lowered resistance to disturbance after encounter-
ing portrayals of violence in movies, radio programs, or newspapers. They show a preoccupation with fears of violent events
and an anticipation of possible violent harm to members of
their families.

Their condition, which we have called *postoperative tension
state*, and which in clinical description comes close to reactive
depression, attains special significance when viewed as an
event affecting a family orbit. In such an orbit, the altered state
of the mother gives rise to anxious concern on the part of the

children, who blame their misconduct for their mother's disturbed condition, or on the part of the husband, who withdraws from interaction with the family, rationalizing his withdrawal as not wishing to disturb the patient. Such disintegration of the family pattern of interaction further increases dismay and tension on the part of the patient and leads to a vicious circle of multiple maladjustments.

Many occasions of severe bereavement demonstrate with striking clarity how the loss of a recently deceased individual, an important link for the interactions of the survivors, forces them into a belated execution of hostile attitudes that first become manifest only after his death. In our recent studies, we have been concerned with the reasons for certain phenomena of incorporation by which the survivor acquires traits or symptoms of the member of the family who has died. A study of interaction patterns of the members of a family in such a situation showed that intolerable hostility between mother and daughter, for instance, might become manifest only after the husband's death.

A young woman of eighteen was brought to the psychiatric outpatient department by her mother because of her stiffness, awkwardness, and inability to get along with anybody, and because the mother "couldn't stand her in the house anymore." The mother had made arrangements for the daughter to attend junior college, but the patient had returned after a few months, and the same series of hostile scenes recurred. The girl had gone to the mother's sister with complaints, further infuriating the mother. It was learned that the husband had died four years earlier, and that the mother had missed him because only he had been able to keep the girl in check.

In the course of psychiatric interviews, the patient revealed that until the father's death theirs had been a happy family, that at the wake the mother had accused the child of lack of affection and had forced her to look into the coffin when the girl was afraid to do so, and that since then she had begun to hate her mother and was now upset about her own hatred. She was afraid she might harm her mother and had often felt unusually strong for a girl. She walked with long, mannish strides and kept herself erect. She had no interest in boys but some attraction to girls, and she made few social contacts. She was preparing to join the Army, since her father had belonged to the Marines. Her overpowering hatred for her mother was her chief emotional concern.

In this case, we may surmise that oedipal rivalry, disguised and still holding the hope of solution while the father lived, flared up in its most primitive form after his death. Either mother or daughter may make a desperate attempt to retain his presence by incorporating his features and acquiring actions previously witnessed as his.

The hostility that is an expression of the disequilibrium in the family after the loss of one of its members may be complicated by the fact that certain features of the role previously assigned to the deceased are now acquired by one of the survivors.

A boy of ten, after the loss of his father, disturbed his mother by outbursts of hostility and provocative behavior. He demanded to be treated with the same respect and affection she had shown for his father and to be trusted with responsibilities requiring more maturity than he possessed. From psychiatric interviews, it became clear that he had no awareness that his claims were not justified. They disappeared only after a severe loss reaction had been worked through in detail.

In another instance, the disturbance in the equilibrium of a family in which the mother had married the brother of a man who had jilted her was also brought to our attention when the son, age eleven, was referred to us through the children's service because of regional ileitis and marked malnutrition.

In the course of interviews with a psychiatric social worker, the mother recognized with considerable guilt that the patient, who had seemed to her to resemble the rejecting brother-in-law, had become the target of strong hostile impulses, of which she had previously been unaware. The boy's interviews with the psychiatrist revealed a fear of desertion by the mother, which had seemed to come true when she left him at the hospital emotionally unprepared for an operation for strabismus. It was then that his anorexia and intestinal disease had started.

On the advice of the social worker, the mother changed her manner toward the boy, who with added psychiatric support, gained twenty-one pounds over a three-month period. During this period, however, the father developed severe anorexia, with a weight loss of thirty-three pounds. He also described a state of apathy and depression with suicidal ruminations. During the course of his discussions with the psychiatrist, the father came to realize that he had become the new target of his wife's hostility, without either of them becoming aware of it. A vicious circle had been set up, in which her nagging and criticism caused him to start eating away from home and keeping late hours, which then led to his being criticized for not showing proper interest in his family. A reconciliation was effected only after the wife had succeeded in having him fire his secretary, to whom he had turned for affection and comfort.

With the father again in the mother's good graces, the little boy began to lose his appetite, complaining of his mother's meanness, and feeling deprived of the signs of her affection which he had been receiving. Once again, he needed psychiatric support.

Meanwhile, the social worker discussed the mother's surplus of hostility with her and the necessity for her to find a target for it outside the family if she were to keep its members safe. She became a floorwalker in a department store, where she had a legitimate opportunity to be aggressive and critical of the

workers under her. Considerably more psychiatric aid was
required before she was able to discharge in interviews the
hostility stemming from her original rejection by the brother-
in-law.

In terms of an epidemiology of emotional disturbances, this
woman might be considered as a carrier of emotional disturbance. It is clear that the increment in hostility and hostile
tension residing in her operated as effectively as a pathogenic
agent as a typhoid colony might operate in a typhoid carrier.
The mode of dissemination of disturbance within the group
and the critical analysis of other forms of dissemination could
easily become a focus of study for the investigator with a
sociological orientation.

CONCLUSION

In conclusion, it seems important to emphasize that we are
still at the very beginnings of an understanding of the complicated processes of the development and discharge of emotions
in the individual, such as the processes involving hostility just
described. In the past, psychiatry has culled most of its information from detailed analyses of isolated individuals. For
purposes of study, they have been too often considered as living
in a social vacuum, with no system of interaction with other
human beings already about them. In therapy, they have been
too often placed in a new institutional group where social
interaction and stimulus was either not afforded them or not
critically observed and controlled. Today, it is to these same
neglected aspects of social interaction and stimulation that we
must turn. We are justified in having great hopes for new
insights if we base our future studies squarely on the emotional
adjustments patients make in the group. The evidence presented here shows something of the basis of this justification.

In making such future studies, we must avail ourselves of

insights borrowed from the social psychologists and anthropologists. With them, and with the objective of psychiatry in mind—the controlling of disorganized, untoward emotional reactions in patients and normal persons alike—we can, before too long, lay the foundations for a preventive psychiatry operating in a community setting.

REFERENCES

Allee, W.C. (1938). *Social Life of Animals.* New York: Norton.

Bard, P. (1934). On emotional expression after decortication with some remarks on theoretical views. *Psychological Review* 41:309-329; 424-449.

Cannon, W.B. (1915). *Bodily Changes in Pain, Hunger, Fear, and Rage.* New York: Appleton.

Dollard, J., et al. (1939). *Frustration and Aggression.* New Haven: Yale University Press.

Freud, S. (1921). Group psychology and the analysis of the ego. *Standard Edition* 18:69-143.

Levy, D. (1941). The hostile act. *Psychological Review* 48:355-361.

Lewin, K., Lippitt, R., and White, R.K. (1939). Patterns of aggressive behavior in experimentally created "social climates." *Journal of Social Psychology* 10:271-299.

Newcomb, T.M. (1947). Autistic hostility and social reality. *Human Relations* 1:69-85.

Parsons, T. (1947). Certain primary sources and patterns of aggression in the social structure of the western world. *Psychiatry* 10:2.

Redl, F. (1942). Group emotion and leadership. *Psychiatry,* 573-96.

Rioch, D.M., Wislocki, G.B., and O'Leary, J.L. (1940). A précis of preoptic hypothalamic and hypophyseal terminology. *Research in Nervous and Mental Diseases* 20.

Rosenzweig, S. (1944). An outline of frustration theory. *Personality and the Behavior Disorders*. New York: Ronald Press.

Part II

Community Mental Health

Introduction to Part II

In 1948 Dr. Lindemann transferred the major portion of his time from the Massachusetts General Hospital to the Harvard University School of Public Health. His colleagues at the Hospital found this move puzzling to say the least, but he was driven by the logic of his quest for methods of preventing mental illness:

The motivational thing was running an out-patient clinic for some twelve years and always getting the late-comers who have had a neurosis usually for some time, having been seen by a lot of people . . . not doctors, but well-meaning, helpful, self-installed caretakers in the community, and then getting a lot of secondary developments which become the bulk of the treatment program, rather than having the initial primary scene which we would like to tackle, and having to go back to it in transference. . . . That was obviously one of the determinants: I wanted to go where in the community traumatic events were taking place, where you could get the

spectrum of reactions and sort out those who were en-
dangered by the situation and those who were not. [Erich
Lindemann, presentation to Visiting Faculty Seminar of
Laboratory of Community Psychiatry, April 21, 1965]

At the School of Public Health he found an ally in Dr. Hugh
Leavell, who thought that the time was ripe for a public health
attack on the problem of mental illness. He succeeded in
having Dr. Lindemann create a Division of Mental Health
within the school and helped him to fulfil his major goal: the
acquiring of a field station in the town of Wellesley where he
could test out his preventive theories.

Dr. Lindemann's new identity as a public health psychiatrist
felt right to him, and he never abandoned it. When he was
called on to succeed Dr. Cobb as Chief of the Psychiatry Service
at the Massachusetts General Hospital in 1954, he met this
transition with the insistence that the hospital should teach
public health concepts and practice public health responsibilities.

The first paper in Part II is theoretical: an attempt to
summarize what Dr. Lindemann already knew about the
"health" part of mental health, and what he would like to find
out about its preconditions in human societies. The second
paper describes salient aspects of the Wellesey Project, and the
third paper takes a common human experience, change of
residence, and traces its mental health consequences under
middle-class-voluntary and working-class-involuntary conditions.

Mental Health—A Dynamic Interpretation

It was a long step from Lindemann's observations of group behavior on a closed ward to the search for factors relevant to mental health and illness in an open community. What constitutes mental health, and how does it manifest itself in community life? Could he, a psychiatrist accustomed to dealing with aberrations of human behavior, say anything meaningful about the healthy personality?

In the paper presented in chapter 6, he tackles this topic by combining the vertical picture of personality development acquired through depth psychology with the horizontal picture of man in society as seen by the sociologist and anthropologist. What emerges is his own ideal image of the mature person.

He also comments on how human societies vary in the kinds and degrees of stress they impose on children and adults, as well as in the resources which they offer to assist in coping. He states as his purpose in going into the Wellesley community a more precise understanding of the way in which these constraints and supports function in a contemporary society.

A paper published by Gordon, O'Rourke, Richardson, and Lindemann (1952) has proposed that we conceive of a *gradient* of health, the ideal case of health being juxtaposed to the fatal case of disease at either extremity of the scale. This proposal challenges us to renew the attempt to define mental health, to find criteria for degrees of mental health, and to look for or design conditions under which it can be studied.

A review of definitions of *mental health* seems to indicate a variety of semantics and concepts, but there also seem to be some common denominators (Senn 1950). All seem to agree that mental health does not mean merely the absence of mental disease, but something positive, approximated by the words, *complete physical, mental, and social well-being.* This is so broad that it describes a value rather than an entity or condition. Freud's simple formulation was that mental health is the capacity to love and to work, implying that productive activity and the capacity for affectionate and considerate relationships to others are ingredients of this value. As one goes further, it is necessary to use a series of sentences; for example, consider the following passage from Rennie and Woodward (1948):

> In very simple terms, a mature and mentally healthy person is one who (1) respects and has confidence in himself, and because he knows his true worth wastes no time proving it to himself and others; (2) accepts, works with, and to a large extent enjoys other people; and (3) carries on his work, his play, and his family and social life with confidence and enthusiasm and with a minimum of conflict, fear or hostility.

A biologically oriented psychiatrist may refer to homeostasis, harmonious integration of functions, and maximum fulfillment of potentialities. A social scientist may, in turn, explain, "To be mentally healthy means to be in harmony with one's culture" (Ahrensberg, personal communication). Erik Erikson (1950) refers to developmental stages of the growing child and emphasizes the timing of basic ingredients in mental health, such as trust rather than distrust, secure autonomy in relations to dependence, and initiative versus guilty inhibition.

And Marie Jahoda (1950), trying to find criteria equally applicable to the individual and the group, says that (1) a mentally healthy individual attempts to master his environment in an active manner rather than adjusting to it with indiscriminate passive acceptance of environmental conditions; (2) he maintains unity of personality, which means a stable internal integration notwithstanding the flexibility of behavior which is necessitated by his active adjustment; and (3) he perceives correctly both the world and its demands on himself and his capacities.

An analysis of all these statements would force us to accept the position that mental health refers to the mode in which an individual copes with the pressures exerted on him by his human environment. The degree of integration between the different parts of the self has been mentioned. The individual's integration with the cultural patterns to which he has to conform and with the growth process with transitions through different levels of function and adjustment is not always smooth and without conflict.

At this point, definitions and descriptions of mental health come close to those of *maturity*, a concept widely used in psychiatry to reflect both mental health and a positive evaluation made by the observer. Maturity as mental health can be either subjective for a given individual or a descriptive reference used by another person, and these two views by no means will always agree. The evaluation of individuals as more or less mature has formed the content of a book by Leon Saul (1947).

My own efforts at clarification of mental health problems

have led to the following formulation: Maturity is reached
through a succession of stages, each appropriate for its level,
each attained with difficulty, and each destined to be reduced to
a residual, often so insignificant that it almost escapes observation but which, nonetheless, becomes integrated into the subsequent stage or stages of development. The residual may
represent a vulnerable point prone to illness or may reassert
itself under conditions of stress at a time when it is inappropriate or out of harmony with the state of growth existing in the
rest of the organism. It is then labeled *immature.*

The term *immature,* as it is used by the scientist, has no value
reference. An immature bird is one that has not yet reached its
full size and strength and its full range of performance. It is
only when former levels of performance appropriate to an
earlier stage of development, and consonant with the level of
growth then attained, persist or reassert themselves at a time
when full maturity in all functions is demanded by the observer
that we speak about immaturity in a somewhat devaluating
sense. In other words, the gradient between the performance
expected from an individual under the circumstances prevailing at that moment, in terms of his social, educational, ethical,
and religious background, and his actual performance is often
described in terms of degrees of maturity.

It should follow from the preceding statements that what we
call mature depends on the expectations impinging on a given
individual from those around him and that the more one asks
of him in terms of level of performance, the greater is the
opportunity for the so-called immaturities to become manifest.
One might even say that the curve of growth in terms of better
and better standards of performance is equalled by a series of
stages of demands placed on an individual because we have
come to expect a certain kind of behavior at each of the different
stages of development.

What we permit a child to do cannot be permitted the adult

because we demand from the latter greater responsibility and entrust to him greater power. But alter the context of demands in which a given person is operating, as in the course of psychoanalysis where everything or almost everything is permitted again as it was once in the days of childhood, or suggest in hypnosis that again it is all right to behave like a child of three, and one will then see a rapid return to ways of acting, thinking, feeling, and speaking characteristic of and appropriate to stages of development supposedly outgrown and long given up.

The balance, the equilibrium, between the demands for excellence in performance and the capacities to operate accordingly to these standards seems to me to be the core of the problem of maturity. The following would be my choice of criteria to characterize a mature person: (1) He should be able to perform the tasks put before him by himself and his society in such a way as to make full use of his capacities without having his efforts hampered by emotional tensions. (2) He should be able to meet the ordinary stresses of life without disintegration or symptom formation, discharging the tension mobilized by the experience in a relief-producing and ultimately constructive manner. (3) He can operate without making others sick, either by depriving them of some element of support or freedom needed for their well-being or by so depleting them by his own demands for love or reward that they have little energy left to carry on their own tasks. (4) He can adapt his perceptions of people and situations to the realities involved, rather than falsifying the picture he forms of them by projecting his own needs into it.

If we are to place individuals along a maturity gradient, we must use the insights acquired from clinical psychiatry to permit us to distinguish between maturity and *pseudomaturity*, which conceals severe developmental flaws under a surface of apparent adequacy. Often the psychiatrist feels that he is confronted by persons whose behavior, although described as ideal by members of the family or friends, turns out under close scrutiny to be possible not because they have mastered the undesirable responses and urges but rather because they have driven underground those energies that otherwise and more normally would be expressed in some form of constructively aggressive behavior. People who seem overly friendly may be wearing a mask that hides hostility or a feeling of emptiness; others adopt the device of martyrdom or willing self-sacrifice in order to control those around them.

If the sex drive is the one that has been repressed, varying degrees of impairment of the capacity for sexual enjoyment may ensue. Such arrested development of drives toward sex or aggression often results from overstimulation—excessive provocation of the drives at a time when the person is too young, too inexperienced to understand or handle them—in which case we speak of a *traumatic experience.*

Such islands of immaturity may be revealed only at the occasion of a crisis or at a time when the legitimate expression of these drives is expected—for example, the exercise of sexuality in marriage or aggressive behavior when the person is faced with the maintenance of standards against an infractor or is the victim of hostile provocation. The absence of satisfaction and the accumulation of tension resulting from such stimulus without appropriate response or transmutation of the energy into a form acceptable for expression may then lead to secondary distortions of the whole personality, or, in other words, to a neurosis.

In the light of our present knowledge, it therefore appears that for parents to be constructive guardians of a growing child, they must be able to tolerate the kind of behavior suited to the various stages of his growth for a long enough time for the child to master that stage and step forward to a higher level of integration, enjoying the satisfactions and attaining complete mastery of the stage-appropriate skills and achievements. If parents prematurely demand from the child behavior that is beyond his age, they must be prepared to have the residues of earlier stages ready to emerge at inappropriate times.

Outward conformity to adult behavior or patterns without genuine mastery of them, their meaning, their occasions of applicability, and their permissible mutations and without transcendence of earlier stages can be achieved by repression—that is, by excluding from consciousness impulses and temptations that with better guidance might be mastered by adequate and reliable control. That which is repressed has not been brought under control; the energy bound up in the repressed item is not available for redirection into constructive endeavors, and the repressed material is quite likely to emerge, distorted and disguised, at awkward and destructive times.

It seems important at this point to elaborate on the positive side of the developmental picture. As we have said, the residues of earlier stages of development may cause trouble. But these very stages of early development—which must be transcended and which, mishandled or cut short, can become noxious foci in the maturing individual—are also the foundations for that richness of expression that must survive and be operative in the healthy child if we want him to be that creative and contributing person whom we desire.

For example, the mature person is not marked by the absence of fear but by his capacity to feel deeply about caring for others and being cared for by them, about the longing for closeness to others, and about the wish to be appreciated as somebody worthwhile in his own right. These feelings, which mark the early stages of development in the small child, must also be felt keenly by the mature adult. The difference between the child and the adult lies in the use to which the feelings are put. That is to say, in the adult the feelings appear in a more complex scheme that has a broader framework of goals and includes more human beings within its scope.

One may further distinguish between the person who has matured with a rich capacity for human relationships and the one who, though well-adjusted, has the sort of *impoverishment* that comes from having had an insufficient number of models to love and emulate during the years of personality formation. The scientist, for example, who is very competent in his laboratory and may appear extremely mature at scientific conferences in exchanging ideas with colleagues may be severely impoverished in all his other human relationships. He may not know how to talk to and feel toward the members of his own family or toward any other person in his community who does not happen to share his language and his preoccupation. He may then retreat from all human contact and wall himself off—an end very easily attained simply by acting as though in one area, at least, he knows so much that he cannot possibly communicate it to lesser mortals.

To prevent such impoverishment, parents must be adequate models themselves and must provide the child with sufficient additional models to allow for flexibility and choice. They must give sufficient affection to allow in the child the emergence of the wish to emulate the loved elder and to be appreciated by him.

Impoverishment may be the consequence of mistaken efforts to give the child the best of all possible environments and upbringings, sparing him exposure to undesirable situations. For instance, the parents who considered the other children on the street bad company and hoped that they themselves would constitute all-sufficient models for their child have prevented him from mastering the social skills necessary for human relations of sufficient diversity. These skills can be obtained only through acquiring and practicing the various modes of behavior suitable for the diverse kinds of human beings whom he will encounter later on. The bad language, the silly jokes, the naughty little stories that the child brings home from the street, and the awkward pronunciation or transitory unpleasing accent may be forbidden and condemned, rather than being identified for the child as more suitable for certain occasions and people than for others.

The rich person, on the contrary, has loved and emulated many people; he has learned to be discriminating about those traits that he has seen in them; he has tested for himself what parts of their behavior and attitudes fit him and in what groups they are appropriate; and he has gradually abandoned those traits not adapted to his course of life. His identifications are varied but harmonious. He has abandoned not only the bad habits of childhood but has also left behind some of those traits that were once highly praised by his elders and that are still desirable for an earlier age.

Such a person does not have to respond to his drives by withdrawing from groups in which he might well participate, to freeze up emotionally and retreat behind a safe wall. Instead, he can respond vigorously and appropriately when occasion arises; and he has a sufficiently safe margin against the accumulation of undue emotional tensions and sufficient alternate avenues of discharge, so that he can enjoy and share the joys of many different kinds of people.

It is one of the limitations of our particular society that often an excessive premium is set on achievement in a limited area, as over against a warm family life, rich friendships and varied activities. Success and public acclaim go to the man who has speeded up the assembly line or who has sold more policies or published more scientific papers. The rewards for maturity in human relationships and the art of living must come from the person's own experience. William Whyte (1943), in *Street Corner Society* provided case histories illustrating the consequences for members of an ethnic group who make one or the other decision.

The definitions of mental health that have been cited stress integration of the individual into his society; but it must at the same time be recognized that to be integrated into one's family, circle of friends, work-team, or any of the groups that form our political and cultural institutions is a sign of maturity *only* to the extent that these groups themselves have a structure expressing the standards of maturity of which we have been speaking for the individual.

In our culture there are inevitable sources of tension and distress that the mature person must be able to handle. There are also some groups so wrong that only a sick man or a distorted one can be content to remain in them and conduct his activities within their frame of reference without pain and dissatisfaction. In other words, the mature person must be integrated into his groups and yet have enough perspective to evaluate them and to become an active source of change within them, so that the group or institution may be prevented from decaying.

Extremely difficult decisions may be required of the mature person when he is forced to take a course of action that appears correct in a wider frame of values but that, for the time being, is contrary to accepted group standards. This has long been recognized as one of the most painful of human predicaments and one most likely to bring retribution from the outraged culture.

To determine the prevalence of mentally healthy or emotionally mature persons in a community and to ascertain their distribution in space and time and fluctuations in this distribution as related to host, agency, and environmental factors would require both a set of measurable criteria and methods of finding with certainty the various levels of mental health. Only a fairly elaborate study of the individual's personality (e.g. White 1948), including his intimate companionships, job performance, and the subjective state of harmony among the segments of the self, can permit an assessment of degrees of mental health. However, limited studies are quite possible with reference to the special performances and the special group relations required by certain social systems such as the family (Bowlby 1951), school (Redl and Wattenberg 1951), army (Ludwig 1947), or industry (Whitehead 1938).

Particular interest is attached to the degree of mental health attained by leaders of the community, both formal leaders and those who influence others in an advice-giving or pace-setting capacity (Adorno et al. 1950). Studies of Hitler and other mass leaders have given striking evidence to the effect that maturity is not a prerequisite for the acquisition of status in the types of groups which thrust these men to the fore.

It is clear that there may be found at all social and economic levels of the population men and women with marked degrees of maturity or mental health and those with impairment of their personality functions. The effect of recent research, such as the study of the "old sergeant syndrome" in the army and the Western Electric Company studies of the productivity of industrial personnel (Whitehead 1938), has been to show that by manipulating the human environment the existing level of individual mental health can be maintained, lowered, or raised within considerable margins. A suitable work-team leads to increased productivity and even the healthy and stable soldier breaks down if more and more members of his emotionally meaningful human environment are removed from him.

In making such studies it soon becomes evident that people differ widely in their requirements for human relationships. The ideally healthy person may have a great variety of constellations compatible with a sense of well-being and productivity, whereas other individuals function well only in close proximity to special types of other persons or are secure only in pair relationships. They appear healthy in the human environment they are able to secure for themselves, but they perhaps become severely decompensated at the time of a critical loss.

Our own studies in bereavement, especially those accompanied by psychosomatic disorders or by personality changes, demonstrate clearly that the emotionally relevant human environment must be included in a study of mental health. Indeed, it is the group of people forming a social unit centered around a given person that must be described in its structure and function as facilitating certain kinds of human interactions and impeding others. There are health-giving, supportive people as well as pathogenic agents.

Social anthropologists also have become increasingly aware of the health problem in different societies and have become interested in prevailing beliefs and attitudes in various cultures, particularly in the rituals that attend the inevitable crises of life. Birth rites, puberty rites, wedding ceremonies, burial rites are examples of community action to deal, in terms of the cultural tradition, with major events in the life of every family. Approaches to cultural diversities and a comparative study of early childhood influences in relation to adult behavior, such as those of Kluckhohn (1944) and Murdock (1949), are important avenues to better understanding of what really affects the process of attaining emotional health. In our Western culture, observation of group behavior of children at nursery-school and elementary-school age, together with a careful scrutiny of the mother's methods of child-rearing, will add much to an understanding of personality development.

What is now known has to remain tentative inference. The amount of evidence is large enough to afford encouragement but not yet quite large enough to produce certainty. We psychiatrists will have to render assistance at the crucial periods of the life cycle, while learning in the greatest detail what constitutes methods of successful mastery of these situations in contrast to those that result in failure. Thus, it will be possible to account more fully for variations in human behavior and experience and to produce those conditions that enable a maximum of mental health for the greatest number of people.

REFERENCES

Adorno, T., Frenkel-Brunswick, E., Levinson, D.J., Sanford, R.N., Aron, B., Levin, M.H., Morrow, W. (1950). The Authoritarian Personality. New York: Harper. 1950.

Ahrensberg, C. Personal communication to the author.

Bowlby, J. (1951). *Maternal Care and Mental Health*. Geneva: Health Organization.

Erikson, E.H. (1950). *Childhood and Society*. New York: Norton.

Gordon, J.E., O'Rourke, E., Richardson, F.L.W., and Lindemann, Erich (1952). The biological and social sciences in an epidemiology of mental disorder. *American Journal of Medical Sciences* 223:316-343.

Jahoda, M. (1950). The healthy personality. In a reprint of a *Report of the House Conference on Child Health*. New York: Josiah Macy Foundation.

Kluckhohn, C. (1944). Navaho Witchcraft, *Papers of the Peabody Museum, Harvard University*, vol. 22, no. 2; Boston: Beacon Press, 1962.

Ludwig, A. (1948). Neuroses in soldiers following prolonged combat exposure. *Bulletin of the Menninger Clinic* 11:15-23.

Murdock, G.P. (1949). *Social Structure*. New York: Macmillan.

Redl, F., and Wattenberg, W. (1951). *Mental Hygiene in Teaching*. New York: Harcourt Brace.

Rennie, T., and Woodward, L. (1948). *Mental Health in Modern Society*. New York: The Commonwealth Fund.

Saul, L.J. (1947). *Emotional Maturity*. Philadelphia: Lippincott.

Senn, M., (1950). *Symposium on the healthy personality*. New York: Josiah Macy Foundation.

White, R.W., (1948). *The Abnormal Personality*. New York: Ronald Press.

Whitehead, T.N., (1938). *The Industrial Worker*. Cambridge: Harvard University Press.

Whyte, W.F. (1943). *Street Corner Society*. Chicago.

The Wellesley Project

It is a paradox that Lindemann regarded the conception and creation of the Wellesley Project as his most significant achievement, whereas he blocked on finishing the book he was supposed to write about it. The following chapter, with his help, has been put together from several reports he made to different groups at different times.

Chapter 7 covers some of the unique features of the experiment: the involvement of citizens in looking at the mental health implications of their collective behavior; consultation with community care-givers, particularly group meetings with the clergy; development of collaboration with two public school systems; and the selection of research projects to illuminate the spectrum of responses to typical crises, such as starting school or entering nurses' training. The description of a clinical service directed toward families rather than individual patients no longer sounds innovative, but such a concept was quite unorthodox at the time it was put into practice.

If the reality of the Wellesley Project fell short of his original *sweeping vision, it nevertheless had a seminal influence on the community mental health movement at home and abroad.* Other contemporary investigators—for example, the Leightons, Rennie, Gruenberg, the Tavistock group in England—were also applying interdisciplinary concepts to the field of mental health. However, in Lindemann's case the life-crisis concept, derived from the bereavement studies, provided a lens through which the array of confusing events occurring in a community could be brought into clear focus, making it possible to design strategies for preventive intervention.*

We chose Wellesley, a suburb of Boston, to develop a community agency to serve the needs of training and research in the field of mental health. It was hoped that the services of such an agency could be made acceptable to the community in a five-year pilot period funded by the Grant Foundation, with the expectation that the citizens would support them from then on. Wellesley was selected because of its willingness to cooperate and because it presented a typical suburban community, with a large, middle-class population, in a metropolitan center. In 1948, when the Project began, Wellesley had approximately 20,000 inhabitants, or 8,000 families.

The services of a mental health agency were conceived as fivefold: (1) a referral resource for emergency situations involving emotional disturbances of one or several members of the community; (2) efforts to detect incipient emotional disorders, and the development of methods of preventive care; (3) to ascertain the distribution of emotional disorders within the community and to develop methods of following the fluctuations in this distribution through time; (4) to become familiar with the activities of various professional and social agencies

*The influence of Lindemann's work on subsequent developments in community mental health will be treated in a forthcoming book by Dr. David Satin.

that had either remedial or preventive implications for mental health and to serve as consultants for the further development of these activities; and (5) participation in community planning in the fields of housing, medical care, education, recreation, and welfare, to bring to bear the influence of mental health principles.

It was expected that an agency to execute these services would provide a field station for the training of individuals in social science and public health, as well as psychiatrists and psychologists. Further, it was hoped that this agency would make accessible a normal population for the purpose of studying the relationship of emotional disturbances to the structure and functions of the social environment.

An interdisciplinary team was assembled, initially including the traditional clinical combination of psychiatrist, psychologist, and psychiatric social worker, together with a research group consisting of social psychologist, sociologist, and anthropologist. A steering committee consisting of Dr. Walter Bauer, Chief of Medical Services at Massachusetts General Hospital; Dr. Hugh R. Leavell of the Harvard School of Public Health; Dr. Samuel Stouffer of the Harvard Laboratory of Social Relations; and Francis Keppel, Dean of the Harvard Graduate School of Education, reflected the interdisciplinary nature of the program.

COMMUNITY COLLABORATION

An *action research* model was adopted; this involved the citizens in planning for services and research through a series of lay committees that used the staff members as resource people. This type of organization had some influence on the choice of research problems, since the citizens objected to certain approaches, but it had the advantage of facilitating work in other areas through their active cooperation.

It would have been relatively easy to enter the town with a ready-made organization, and with a program tailored to our research aims. In that case, however, our team would have been likely to prove a foreign body in community life. It would also have been quite possible to defer any clear-cut structure of our activities indefinitely, waiting for community needs to show themselves spontaneously. Instead, we tried to stimulate the community to focus its attention on urgent problems that needed to be investigated and planned for, hoping at the same time to accommodate our research interests.

We therefore asked the Community Council to appoint an executive committee of fifteen citizens; eight were businessmen or other prominent laymen with an interest in mental health, whereas the other seven had some professional concern with problems of human relationships. This executive committee helped us to design a system of joint staff-citizen committees to review present policies and procedures in seven areas of community life and to define those situations in which our group could be most helpful. The following committees were envisaged: family services, clergy, schools, physicians, industry and occupational problems, recreation and neighborhoods, and ecological problems. The last-named committee reflected an interest in knowing what section of the population was particularly susceptible to mental disorders—a common belief being that the mobile section, the new arrivals and those who moved frequently within the town, would show a higher incidence than the old settlers.

It was in these committees that the service program was developed and that specific research enterprises were discussed and cleared. No activity emanated solely from the mental health agency. Particular emphasis was placed on the citizens' responsibility for the right kind of publicity and on their capacity to interpret the enterprise to their fellow townsmen.

CLINICAL SERVICE

Our aim was not to form a clinical facility for long-term treatment of a small number of cases but rather to provide a mental health agency to assist families and other types of groups in times of emergency and help them design a program of action at the most suitable level. Who in the group was "the patient" was often an unanswered question: The emphasis was on pathological relationships, as other individuals found to have a pathogenic effect on the so-called patient might be much more important than the person with whom the initial complaint was concerned. An alteration of the system of human relationships to which the alleged patient was exposed might turn out to be useful not only to him but also to a number of other members of the group who did not happen to present themselves as patients. This meant that there had to be a core of traditional therapeutic facilities, but attention had to be distributed to the various members of the family and of other social groups; referral to other treatment sources would often have to be facilitated, and effective therapeutic contact would have to be limited to the immediate crisis, followed by a plan of action designed to forestall the recurrence of the pathogenic circumstances.

We became interested in the circumstances under which conditions that have been tolerated for some time are suddenly perceived as *pathological* and are then the cause of a further disturbance in the equilibrium of a group. The following case illustrates this point:

A fourteen-year-old boy was referred as the culprit in a noisy scene in which another boy was beaten up and sexual assault was involved. Both were members of a youth organization that took great pride in the moral standing of its members. Investigation showed 1) that the culprit and certain other boys had engaged in similar activities before without arousing the ire of the adults; 2) that there was a feud between the fathers of the boys involved in the encounter, based on personal and business rivalries; 3) that the director of the group had taken a special interest in the culprit, trying to demonstrate that poorly adjusted boys can be helped by appreciative guidance; 4) that this director, a recent arrival in town, had become an object of hostility and resentment on the part of the members of the adult group to which the two fathers belonged; and 5) that the scandal over the situation was effective in driving the director to resign from his position. The equilibrium of the total group was such that the needs of the adults facilitated and brought into focus the juvenile delinquency. The hostility of the parents was acted out by the boys, and their activities, in turn, became useful weapons for the elders.

Another example concerns accusations of sexual misconduct against an aged custodian of a school building. These accusations were effective in leading to his resignation.

Investigation showed that five girls, all in early puberty, who had played with the jolly old man "innocently" up to that time, had recently been warned at home about the dangerous implications of playing with men. The leader of the girls, from an ethnic Italian household with close kindship ties, was warmly attached to another old man, her grandfather, who continued to pay keen attention to her against the objections of her mother. The fate of the custodian, the worries of the building administration, and the propensities of the girls toward hysterical neurotic development all had to be taken into account for adequate treatment of the situation.

CONSULTATION WITH CARE-GIVERS

Thorough acquaintance with the mode of operation and the set of values that determined the action of clergymen in different denominations, educators in the public school system, medical practitioners, and law enforcement personnel was required in order that we might predict the ideal mode of handling a situation and suggest only such motivations as would be compatible with the goodwill and tolerance of the various professional groups. It became necessary, therefore, to have meetings at regular intervals with each profession to compare points of view and its folklore about problems and emotional disorders and to translate from one jargon to the other the major assumptions and customary lines of management.

From the bereavement studies it had become clear that the clergy, as one of the care-giving professions in the community, could make a significant contribution to mental health. The Clergy Committee constituted a work group that included the ministers of the various churches, one of the Catholic priests, and the rabbi of the small Jewish group. A total of twelve clergymen met first at biweekly and later at monthly intervals to discuss their concerns with the emotional problems of their parishioners, using a psychiatrist and a sociologist of the Human Relations Service as resource persons. The sessions served to compare the types of emotionally disturbed individuals and families that turn to the minister for help with those usually seen by psychiatrists. The methods of assistance the clergyman has developed to render service at the times of the major life crises—birth, puberty, marriage, childbearing, and death—were considered and compared with the procedures now labeled psychotherapy. The points at which a clergyman would hesitate to make a referral to a psychiatrist, and the points of reluctance of a psychiatrist to share certain problems with the clergy, were analyzed.

The discussions with the clergy demonstrated a sequence of stages that turned out to be typical for other professional groups with which we consulted. The first requests were for permission to refer to the Service persons who were definitely sick, and whose care was beyond the resources of the clergy. A considerable number of patients with psychoses and severe neuroses, who the clergyman had been carrying because of a lack of psychiatric resources, were now brought to our Human Relations Service, as the mental health agency was called, for evaluation. Commitment to mental hospitals from the Service was avoided; in the case of a few patients with whom this was necessary, the referring clergyman was informed that local physicians could help with this procedure.

A number of other patients with chronic disorders were discussed in an effort to understand why previous psychiatric treatment had failed, so that the clergyman could accept the lack of improvement and not blame himself for his failure to help the patient. The clergy, in fact, were dealing quite successfully with a number of emotionally disturbed persons among their parishioners; some problems they felt they could handle; others they felt obliged to continue in pastoral care even though these persons became annoying and demanded excessive time and effort. In such instances, it became the task of the mental health professional to review with the clergyman the specific situation in which the person was functioning, appraising the care he was getting from his family and the understanding he was receiving in the neighborhood. We became impressed with the presence in some neighborhoods of trusted citizens who were quite effective in creating in the surrounding families a more positive attitude toward a person who has only partly recovered from a mental illness. We began to speak of them as "informal leaders," and to reckon with them as one of the care-giving groups.

Out of these discussions evolved a second type of work with the clergy which later was called *mental health consultation.* (Caplan 1970). The parishioner who presents a problem is not brought up for referral, but the clergyman wishes to have advice concerning his own attitude and procedures with such a person and his family. Part of these discussions dealt with the nature of emotional disorders and adjustment problems. However, it soon became possible to evaluate with the clergyman the reasons why such a parishioner became a problem at this particular time and to review aspects of the clergyman's own attitudes and convictions that made it particularly difficult to deal with this parishioner's problem.

There naturally evolved a series of discussions concerning the boundary between pastoral care as a religious activity and psychotherapy as a form of medical treatment. It seemed unwise for the development of a mental health program to have clergymen become psychotherapists, and equally unwise for psychiatrists to deal with issues of religious values. For the clergyman to have his proper function in the community, it would continue to be necessary to view the behavior of his parishioners and their families in the light of the religious values and ethos of his church. Central to the clergyman's role are issues of belonging and not belonging, of guilt and forgiveness, and of faith concerning the ultimate nature of the universe, as well as many questions relating to the contribution each member of the congregation makes to the whole group. The psychiatrist, on the basis of his scientific competence in the fields of biology and psychology, can add diagnostic and therapeutic understanding of the patient's psychological functioning. He can map out the limits of the patient's capacity to adjust, and can point to untapped resources that might be mobilized by psychotherapy.

After much complaint about the lack of genuine assistance, which clergymen often feel they fail to get in connection with parishioners whom they refer to psychiatrists for office consultation, the discussion began to shift to broader aspects of the function of church or temple in the community and to the internal organization of religious institutions. In addition to the pastor's function as preacher and visitor to members of the

congregation, he organizes an elaborate system of group activities and rituals relating to significant periods in the life
cycle of the parishioners. There are the ceremonies of baptism,
confirmation, marriage, and memorial services; and there are
the institutions of "Sunday School," young people's associations, group meetings for married couples, and activities for
the older members of the congregation.

The clergymen became concerned about the significance of
their ceremonial procedures for parishioners at such highly
emotional moments as weddings and funerals. A whole series
of discussions evolved concerning problems of cooperation
with the physicians in the last months of the life of a patient
with incurable illness. How much should a patient be told, and
how much should the family know? How could both be helped
to master the problems of death and bereavement? A joint
meeting with the group of physicians in Wellesley brought out
striking differences in the practice and ritual of different
churches and in the specific values that would be stressed at the
time of such crisis. It had become manifest by this time that the
regular meetings of the clergy at the Human Relations Service
provided an opportunity for them to communicate with each
other across the boundaries of their denominations and to gain
information about each other's orientation, which furthered
their understanding of common problems in the mental health
field.

Questions relating to group life in the church led to requests
for speakers from the Human Relations Service to address the
various groups—for example, to address a group of adolescents
on sex and marriage. It also led to a discussion of the choice of
leaders for such groups, in terms of their qualifications and
supervision. One problem was how to deal with the wish of
volunteers to have a role for which they do not appear suited.
Criteria for personnel selection in terms of maturity and relative freedom from conflicts needed clarification. Group dy-

namics issues, such as the size of the group and the nature of its activities, were discussed with a steady rise in interest.

Finally, these discussion led to a growing awareness on the part of the professionals of the limitations of existing knowledge, and of the many opportunities for joint inquiry and problem-solving with regard to regular sequences to be anticipated in the evolution of emotional disturbances. For example, the clergyman may notice at what stage in the marriage a couple considers divorce, and under what circumstances, and he may consider whether this outcome could have been predicted at the time of premarital counseling. Or again, how can one predict at the time of the funeral the likelihood of a pathological reaction to a loss? In view of the need for systematic study, there was review of the training of clergymen and a consideration of possible additions to their undergraduate and graduate curriculum. There was eagerness to contribute to mental health research: Could parishioners be used as informants, or as participants in mental health screening operations? It had to be made clear that the selection of a survey population is a complicated problem, in which the enthusiam of the participants is only one small factor.

The experience of the Clergy Committee illustrates the four types of consideration and joint endeavor that can be expected to emerge in the course of interprofessional mental health work: (1) direct referral to the psychiatric professions for care; (2) consultation about problems remaining in the care of the nonpsychiatric professional; (3) discussion of institutional arrangements and routines that the latter have developed in order to strengthen personal growth and avoid emotional difficulties; and (4) joint inquiry and planning with respect to factors that seem to contribute to good or poor outcomes, both at the individual and at the institutional level.

The role of a mental health agency in providing a neutral meeting ground for discussing common concerns, thus helping community agencies to build adequate channels of communication rather than existing in a state of competitive isolation, also became clear to us. Prior to the formation of the Clergy Committee there had been no vehicle for regular interaction of the clergymen as a group. Similarly, the Family Services Committee brought together the persons who were engaged in welfare work on a professional or voluntary basis: The Department of Public Welfare, the Salvation Army, the Junior Service League, the Visiting Nurse Association (VNA), and the Friendly Aid Association reviewed their respective areas of concern and compared their methods. An attempt was then made to formulate the way in which our Service could become coordinated with these existing agencies. Regular case consultations were scheduled with the combined staffs of the Friendly Aid and the VNA, and were considered by them to be a valuable addition to their effectiveness. However, our original plan to review their case records in order to determine the incidence of mental disorders met with resistance and was abandoned in favor of a questionnaire-type survey of mental health "predicaments."

In our contacts with the Friendly Aid Association, we became aware of the strong need of middle-class women to use a family agency for volunteer work, giving them a socially useful outlet for their energies and fostering companionship and pride in making a contribution. The growing professionalization of the agency progressively deprived them of this opportunity, resulting in unmistakeable hostility toward the professional workers. It was also striking to observe the differences in values, goals, and methods between the nursing and social work professions. Inevitable mutual tensions prevented effective collaboration until a forum had been provided for comparing attitudes and discharging aggressive feelings against the members of the other profession.

The public school system became the most important area of

consultation and joint planning. The town's Mental Health Committee, which had sponsored our arrival, was particularly concerned about high-school pregnancies. It seemed that a program of mental health maintenance carried out with educators not only would contribute significantly to the overall mental health of the community but also would further our research interests. The school system, like industrial and military organizations, is a place where groups of individuals meet regularly for long periods of activity subject to well-defined rules of interaction; therefore, studies in connection with such systems promise reliable data.

An early concern in the community before our arrival had been the prevention of juvenile delinquency. Efforts had been made to furnish the teachers with a checklist that would make it easy for them to identify and report about pupils who might be in need of psychiatric help. One of the tasks of the joint Committee on Schools was to review these efforts. The committee concluded that spotty reports about conspicuous behavior traits of a given child or group of children would be of little value unless observations of teachers could be correlated with a consistent body of data collected about the child from the moment he enters school. It was agreed that an examination of the emotional condition of the child comparable with and correlated with the physical examination required for entry into kindergarten was an urgent need. In other words, a review of emotional adjustment would have to be part and parcel of a comprehensive health examination. Thus began the experimentation with various methods of prekindergarten mental health screening, which became a focus for important research and led to the development of the Preschool Checkup, a model preventive program.

Joint planning of a preschool screening program brought the Human Relations Service into a collaborative, and sometimes competitive, relationship with the public school system;

hence, it ensured a high degree of interaction with the top administrative levels and stimulated constant questioning of, and joint evaluation of, mental health principles and methods. Gradually, a service program was worked out that included making regular consultation by our staff and trainees available to classroom teachers, special personnel, and administrators regarding mental health problems of pupils or groups of pupils. Families of pupils throught to be in need of psychiatric help were referred to the agency for clinical evaluation. Our staff also took part in various school-initiated programs of in-service training and in sessions to feed back the results of our research.

A second public school program was developed in the neighboring town of Weston. In this case the consultations were centered around the program of the Guidance Department, whose director, Charles Cummings, was interested in learning whether social and emotional problems becoming manifest in high school pupils could have been detected and dealt with prophylactically at the elementary level. A social worker from our staff was assigned to visit the families of elementary children considered by the teachers to have problems. This pattern was different from the one developed in Wellesley.

A third avenue of access to educators was provided by the nursery schools, which had assumed an important role in this middle-class community. One of them furnished the subjects for a study of the management of children's aggression. Later, it was possible to bring together the staffs of the various nursery schools for monthly meetings on mental health topics, much as we had done with the clergymen from different churches.

Optimal relationships with community care-givers were found to depend on sensitivity to their preferred modes of interaction. Not all of them were comfortable with the psychiatric model of sitting down and talking. Each profession, as well as subgroups of professionals in a given building or agency, had its own mores about when, where, how long, and with whom to exchange information. The town's physicians, for example, found it extremely hard to fit committee meetings into their busy schedules. Their cooperation took the form of referrals to our clinical service, which were then handled as consultations. After several years a Balint-type group was conducted for pediatricians in response to their increasing interest in the psychological aspects of their work. One of the members of this group, Dr. William Brines, then served a term as Chairman of the Board of Directors of our agency. The police also contacted us sporadically in connection with crises that they thought had mental health implications.

INTERDISCIPLINARY COOPERATION

In all of these efforts at collaboration with care-givers, as well as with the broader issue of community acceptance, the help of the social scientists on the staff was invaluable. They provided the conceptual frame of reference that made it possible to enter local institutions without disturbing the prevailing hierarchy and role distribution in the social system. They also knew how to ascertain for each segment of the community the type and degree of deviation from its social norms that would be judged as requiring clinical intervention. Since referrals to the clinical service were accepted on the principle that groups rather than individuals would be evaluated, our clinicians needed to be appraised of the institutional and cultural features of such groups. Thus the decision to operate the agency with an interdisciplinary team was justified. This was in contrast with the model used by Leighton, who separated clinical and research teams to avoid contamination of research results. We felt that at this exploratory stage of the inquiry, maximum participation in the program by all disciplines would be desirable.

Ideally, the entire staff—those whose primary role was to see patients and those who came equipped to carry out investigations—were faced with the dual task of establishing a therapeutic service and of extending clinically relevant knowledge. However, interdisciplinary work turned out to be no easy task. The conceptual frames of reference of the anthropologist and sociologist, and the factual content of their fields, can be shared relatively easily with the psychiatrist and psychologist. There are, however, at least four major obstacles to cooperation.

1. The psychiatrist is likely to remain patient-centered and focused on intrapsychic phenomena, even if he wishes to contribute to social science. The statements of the social scientist may appear to him as superficial generalities that lack pertinence for the individual case requiring care.

2. The psychiatrist usually has an optimistic bias, and is inclined to center his attention on a central theme, disregarding and underplaying a number of partial variables. The social scientist is likely to see the importance of many variables. His bias is pessimistic insofar as effectual manipulation is concerned, and he is continually reminding the psychiatrist how slow and tedious is the process of securing scientifically conclusive knowledge.

3. There are also problems of status hierarchy in a system with a clinical core. And there are rivalries over techniques of interviewing hallowed by tradition in the different disciplines.

4. There is finally the basic orientation around "the problem." The psychiatrist wishes to find a basis for a plan of action, whereas the social scientist wishes to elucidate a state of affairs for the purpose of greater theoretical clarification.

It is necessary to get acquainted, to know each other much better than was originally thought required, and to have sympathy with one another's value orientations. It is also desirable to develop work-teams of different internal structures, giving each related discipline the opportunity for leadership. Agreements reached by the conference method may turn out to be hollow and an uncertain basis for further planning unless these motivational factors are taken into account.

RESEARCH

The concepts on which research planning was based were those of

1. The emotionally relevant human environment
2. Frequency and duration of social interactions
3. Role distribution within the social system
4. Equilibrium and disequilibrium at times of crisis

Central assumptions were as follows: Given a situation leading to disequilibrium of a social system—either a family or other social organization—readaptation will be required from the members of the group. These responses may be adaptive or maladaptive. Responses that appear adaptive at first may, on closer study, be found to represent precursors of later disturbance.

The starting point for these studies was a review of reactions to severe bereavement, in which it was possible to distinguish, on the one hand, "normal," effective grief work and, on the other hand, morbid types of adjustment—including psychotic, psychosomatic, and psychoneurotic reaction types and also certain forms of personality change that merely reduced the survivor's scope of functioning.

It seemed important to find other situations of crisis or transition which would make it possible to study the reactions of individuals with different personality structures, and their ways of mastering the attendant problems. One such crisis was repeatedly referred to our clinical service—namely, the return to the family of a mental hospital patient. This situation provided a model for clinical investigation in a community, according to which not the referred individual but the group of which he is a member becomes the object of service and study. Service records were developed to collect data on the condition of the social system, the "emotionally relevant environment" of the ex-patient. We also studied the role redistribution that would have to take place in order to reabsorb the returning member, thus documenting why such people so often become sick again at short notice. We collected a number of case studies in which we could clearly show what happened in the family to make it impossible for that member to be reintegrated.

To do systematic research on large portions of the population, however, it was necessary to motivate various segments of the community to cooperate. It was possible to win over a group of families with nursery-school-age children and a large percentage of families with children entering public kindergarten to volunteer as subjects, thereby helping to promote understanding of varieties of adjustment to social stress.

The nursery school studies were designed by the social scientists on the team to explore aspects of American middle-class family life that may be relevant for mental health. They described the way in which individual families or family members master a specific problem in normal child development—namely, the control of aggressive behavior. Naegele's study (1951) elicited information from mothers of children in nursery school as to how they typically defined and managed aggression and hostility in themselves, their children, and their husbands; and this information was related to other data on the social structure of these families. A similar study by Aberle and Naegele (1952) of the fathers of these same families described the distribution of the father's interest between work and family concerns and contributed to an understanding of the way in which the nursery-school-age boy becomes the focus of paternal concern relative to his eventual occupational success, while his sister remains relatively free of such concern.

Studies of children and their families at the transition point of entry into kindergarten focused on the adaptation required of family members when the child leaves home and goes to school, as well as on the child's own patterns of coping with a new life experience (Gruber 1954, E.B. Lindemann and Ross 1955, McGinnis 1954). It was possible through a series of group meetings with parents, as in the case of the bereavement studies, to delineate a typical course of anticipation, upset, or disequilibrium followed by readjustment, as experienced by these families (Klein and Ross 1958). A free pre-school checkup, offered to the community and carried out at the Human Relations Service each year, has afforded an opportunity for interviewing mothers individually and seeing the child in a play situation, in an attempt to ascertain from a relatively brief contact what type of emotional adjustment prevails within the family orbit and what situations the child is probably going to meet successfully in contrast to those in which he is probably going to fail. By creating a simulated crisis—the child's separation from his mother at our agency—we hope to be able to prognosticate reactions to subsequent crises. It was hoped that experience gained over a number of years in this voluntary preschool assessment would eventually lead to population-wide surveys that could identify and bring preventive services to bear on children who are vulnerable to difficulties in school or to later breakdown (Klein and E.B. Lindemann 1964).

A similar cross-sectional study of transition was made in the School of Nursing of the Newton-Wellesley Hospital. This study showed the hazards encountered by first-year nursing students as they attempted to embrace a professional role (Rosenberg and Fuller 1955). The dropout rate of the first-year class was significantly lowered by providing mental health assistance to the students through group discussions. We learned that only to a limited degree do student nurses have the problem of cumulative acquisition of information, but to a much larger degree they experience problems relating to mastery of a professional role and assumption of a new identity (Rosenberg and Fuller 1957). Here again is an example of entering the mental health field not in order to prevent a specific disease but to deal with a variety of untoward consequences of a maladaptive encounter with a situation—such as dropping out of college for a reason that is not fully understood or choosing a career for which one is poorly suited.

The development of longitudinal studies, in which children can be followed from the preschool period or earlier all the way through high school and beyond, was a goal of our community work, but it proved difficult to achieve. As a first step, we instituted follow-up surveys of children who attended the preschool checkup and made use of teacher and parent observations in order to check on our staff's predictions regarding their ability to adapt successfully to the school environment (E.B. Lindemann et al. 1967).

We also approached the problem of the distribution of emotional disorders within the community with classical epidemiological methods. The assumption was made that there exists in every community a manifest case load known to the professional agencies, as well as a hidden case load of emotionally disturbed individuals who are known only to themselves, to their families, or to outside institutions. There was also the assumption that the distribution of disturbances was to be understood in terms of differential strain in various geographical areas corresponding to various regions of the social structure. The Wellesley community, which superficially appeared homogeneous, was actually found to be made up of contrasting neighborhoods, or sections, with demarcations which were meaningful to the residents and were subsequently shown to be significant in terms of mental health service and research (Lewis 1956). On the other hand, the pattern of referral of "predicaments" with mental health implications to the various professions in town was found to be somewhat haphazard. It was also established that in comparison with a low-income area of Roxbury, Wellesley tended to keep a larger proportion of its psychotic patients at home rather than hospitalize them (Kaplan, Reed, and Richardson 1956). An extension of these epidemiological considerations to the State level was facilitated when Dr. Warren Vaughan, a member of our staff, was put in charge of the Massachusetts Department of Mental Health survey of State psychiatric institutions and clinics (Vaughan, Conwell, and Kaplan 1953). A study of the social and emotional impact of moving into Wellesley, or moving from one neighborhood to another within the town, was carried out by a staff anthropologist, L. Thoma, and is summarized in chapter 8.

In conclusion, the Wellesley Project represented an early attempt to develop a community mental health center. The research program, rather than being a unitary project, consisted of a series of individual projects developed in response to the challenge of problems arising from its service activities. Over a fifteen-year period, about 2,000 families became known to the Human Relations Service. Emotional disorders referred for assessment ranged from frank psychoses to psychoneuroses, delinquency, and psychosomatic conditions. In addition to direct clinical service on a short-term basis to individuals and families, an elaborate program of consultation was carried out with the Wellesley and Weston public school systems, the Newton-Wellesley Hospital School of Nursing, and with clergy, medical practitioners, social agencies, and law-enforcement personnel. The agency became a field station for community mental health training for graduate students in psychiatry, psychology, and social work—supported by grants from the National Institute of Mental Health, administered by the Massachusetts General Hospital.

We were able to create a mental health agency that fit well with the expectations and concerns of the citizens of a suburban middle-class community: the advancement and success of their children, the control of deviance and failure, and the early discovery of possible impairment of health. Members of the community were able to plan cooperatively and to develop their own program, using us as resource persons.

REFERENCES

Aberle, D.F., and Naegele, K.D. (1952). Middle class fathers' occupational role and attitudes toward children. *American Journal of Orthopsychiatry* 22:366-378.

Caplan, G. (1970). *The Theory and Practice of Mental Health Consultation*. New York: Basic Books.

Gruber, S. (1954). The concept of task-orientation in the analysis of play behavior of children entering kindergarten. *American Journal of Orthopsychiatry* 24:326-335.

Kaplan, B., Reed, R.B., and Richardson, F.L.W., Jr. (1956). A comparison of the incidence of hospitalized and non-hospitalized psychoses in two communities. *American Sociological Review* 21:472-479.

Klein, D.C., and Lindemann, Elizabeth. (1964). Approaches to pre-school screening. *Journal of School Health* 34:365-373.

Klein, D.C., and Ross, A. (1958). Kindergarten entry: a study of role tranisition. In *Orthopsychiatry and the School,* ed. M. Krugman, pp. 60-69. New York: American Orthopsychiatric Association.

Lewis, G. (1956). A technique in social geography for the delimitation of urban residential subregions. Unpublished dissertation, Harvard University.

Lindemann, Elizabeth and Ross, A. (1955). A follow-up study

of a predictive test of social adaptation in preschool children. In *Emotional Problems of Early Childhood,* ed. G. Caplan, pp. 79-93. New York: Basic Books.

Lindemann, Elizabeth, et al. (1967). Predicting school adjustment before entry. *Journal of School Psychology* 6:24-42.

McGinnis, M. (1954). The Wellesley Project program of preschool emotional assessment. *Journal of Psychiatric Social Work* 23:135-141.

Naegele, K.D. (1951). Some problems in the study of aggression in middle-class American families. *Canadian Journal of Economics and Political Science* 27:65-75.

Rosenberg, P., and Fuller, M. (1955). Human relations seminar: a group work experiment in nursing education. *Mental Hygiene* 39:406-432.

——— (1957). Dynamic analysis of the student nurse. *Group Psychotherapy* 10:22-37.

Vaughan, W.T., Jr., Conwell, M., and Kaplan, B. (1953). Survey of community psychiatric resources in Massachusetts. Conducted by Harvard University School of Public Health, Department of Mental Health. East Gardner, Massachusetts.

Chapter 8

Moving as a Crisis

Several factors influenced Lindemann's decision to study the mental health consequences of relocating the West End population in order to build high-rise apartment and office buildings. One motivation, emphasized in this chapter, was to extend the scope and usefulness of his crisis theory by comparing the ways in which two different types of populations met the challenge of moving.

Another consideration, deriving from his own move from the School of Public Health back to the Massachusetts General Hospital to become Stanley Cobb's successor, was the wish to sound the theme that was to characterize his tenure of that position—namely, the relevance of the human environment for mental health and illness. The people of the West End and the M.G.H. had existed in a mutually meaningful relationship; their separation through the renewal program could not fail to have significance for both parties and might plausibly lead to an increase of morbidity on the part of the relocatees. To ascertain this it would be necessary to include social scientists in the mental health team, just as had been the case in the Wellesley Project.

Lindemann had also experienced a broadening of his interest in the effect that government policies may have on community coping patterns through his semiannual participation in Dr. Leonard Duhl's "Space Cadets," or National Institute of Mental Health Committee on Social and Physical Environmental Variables as Determinants of Mental Health. He was greatly stimulated by the thinking in this group, which included lawyers and city planners as well as social scientists. It was thanks to Duhl's advice and encouragement that he applied for and received a five-year grant from the National Institute of Mental Health to study the effects of urban renewal on the West End population.

In connection with our studies on bereavement as a possible precursor of certain forms of somatic illness, we had become interested in the bereaved state itself and had become convinced that transitional states—such as grief, a condition between health and illness—should be understood more thoroughly in order to prevent maladaptive responses by timely intervention.

We developed a series of assumptions about precipitous change in social systems that might constitute a hazardous situation for the persons involved because such change often demands the mobilization of responses not available in the ordinary response repertory and requires a reorganization both of the social system and of the intrapsychic organization. We began to speak about crisis behavior as maladaptive or well-adaptive, began to separate defensive reactions from coping mechanisms, and tried to find a variety of transition points in the life cycle at which the reactions and choices could be observed and at which some clues could be gained about factors in the social system determining the outcome.

One such transition point is change of residence. It was

possible in Wellesley, a suburb of Boston, and in the West End, an urban working-class neighborhood, to study contrasting conditions under which moving from one home to another in a different community takes place.

The problems associated with mobility first came to our attention in the course of seeing clinical patients from the Wellesley community. The middle-class American's tendency to uproot himself and his family has come to appear inevitable, often desirable, and, for those who are climbing the economic ladder, vitally necessary. Nevertheless, in spite of the positive value placed by the culture on moving, there are many who find it difficult, even when the move brings higher status, a more attractive environment, and better schools. It was apparent that the highly mobile pattern of certain segments of the Wellesley population included certain hazards, both for individuals and for the community.

Another kind of mobility is that which is imposed on a total population by circumstances beyond their control, such as the mass evacuations taking place in wartime or on a smaller scale, through the planned demolition and rebuilding of city neighborhoods. The so-called urban renewal of the West End of Boston in the 1950s gave us the opportunity to compare the effects of forced mobility on the mental health of a working-class population with the observations we had made in Wellesley.

Early in our acquaintance with Wellesley, our attention was drawn to the fact that many new families were moving into town, imposing strains on its social structure and administration. Our citizen collaborators hoped that we would find a preponderance of pathology among the newcomers. Instead of looking for cases in the incoming population, we explored the meaning of the transitional experience, both for the newcomers and for those who received them. Interviews revealed the complexity and variety of processes which this middle-class community developed to integrate and control the newcomer. They also pointed to the negative impact that moving, in some instances, can have on mental health, ranging from disruption of meaningful individual and family ties to actual scapegoating of families perceived as deviant in their new surroundings.

Sometimes the family has moved several times and has acquired certain skills in facilitating the change. Nevertheless, it often means an unanticipated crisis for one or more members of the family, resulting from the disruption of relations with close friends, schoolmates, and teenage peer groups. The family as a whole faces a difficult period as it adjusts to a new lifestyle and establishes new ties. Success or failure in coping with the attendant stress is influenced by the extent to which the host community aids in the assimilation process.

Communities differ widely in the manner and degree in which they anticipate such difficulties and reduce the timeless hostility of the old versus the new. They may wish to facilitate or to impede the successful adaptation of newcomers, and they will in any case have criteria for those they wish to accept. A survey of newly arrived families in Wellesley during 1953 and 1954 showed that real estate agents functioned to select those who were deemed acceptable to the town and could be expected to be readily integrated. These were preferably persons of white Anglo-Saxon Protestant background, with appropriate education, job status, and manners. Persons of different ethnic origin were discouraged from seeking homes or were shown undesirable dwellings. After this selection process, once the family had moved in there followed a series of efforts on the part of local businesses, the schools, and the churches to facilitate acquaintance and integration. Social contacts could be procured through a large variety of clubs, arranged in a hierarchy that provided membership first at the lower levels with a gradual rise in prestige and influence in town affairs.

Clinical observations showed that women in particular felt

unhappy unless they were soon admitted to organizations in which they could begin to have a meaningful role in the community. There was strong pressure on both men and women to participate in such activities as committee work and fund-raising drives, and families that did not participate could become targets for a form of scapegoating—namely, noninclusion in social events. In such cases, the children often became conspicuous as troublemakers, and it was their problems that brought the parents to the mental health agency. Our task was then to help the family to understand why they were being scapegoated and how to undo this process. Emotional distress was found more often in children than in adults, since little thought had been given to the crisis of transition because of new surroundings they faced at their respective age levels.

Among the women whom we tried to help, we found that the opportunity for some quasi-intimate contacts beyond the immediate family was an important need. This became a major theme when we studied the dispersion of families from an inner-city neighborhood, with its close kinship and friendship ties, into the more impersonal suburbs.

The West End Study centered on the working-class population of the West End of Boston at the occasion of an *urban renewal,* or slum clearance project, that required the relocation of approximately 2,500 families. In Wellesley, the research emphasis was on healthy or unhealthy adaptive patterns of individual newcomers and on the processes, various and complex, that a middle-class suburb had developed to integrate and control them. We now saw the opportunity to study a large population facing a common predicament—an arbitrarily imposed crisis that meant leaving its habitat and finding new homes in unfamilar environments. We wished to learn whether variations in adaptation to this crisis might be ascribed to the following special factors: that mobility was forced and not chosen; that individuals faced a common challenge; and, finally, that the resources, emotional and material, were those peculiar to a working-class population.

Unlike a large number of studies which have dealt with rates of mental disorder associated with migration and change of habitat (Murphy 1965, Eaton), the West End Study was not primarily an epidemiological survey. Its theoretical focus was influenced by recent studies of coping behavior by Hamburg and his co-workers, who analyzed typical adaptive patterns in a variety of severe stress situations—such as freshman adjustment to college, response to life-threatening injuries, and anticipation of losing a child with an incurable illness (Coelho and Hamburg 1963, Hamburg 1953, Chodhoff, Friedman, and Hamburg 1964). According to these observations, as well as to those on bereavement responses by Engel (1961), Schmale (1958), and ourselves, we could expect the adaptive behavior of a community that was losing its existence *as* a community to include certain cognitive components, such as the search for information; certain affective components, such as mourning and anxiety; and special types of future-oriented behavior, representing rehearsals of the new situation or testing out acceptable patterns of encounter with the human environment.

Furthermore, we expected this study to throw additional light on the shared values and defenses of a working-class population. The rich descriptive material elicited by Oscar Lewis (1966) about Mexican and Puerto Rican lower-class communities had provided us with the picture of their special "culture of poverty." Their historical place in the larger society, their shared fate in the struggle to improve their standard of living in the face of severe odds, and repeated experiences of frustration and failure seem to be determinants of a highly valued style of life, vigorously defended against outside interference and characterized by inner coherence and mutual help. We wanted to search for such patterns in our target population of 10,000 relocatees and especially to learn about cultural factors that might be related to various forms of illness and disease or to other problems requiring agency assistance.

The importance of such an inquiry was recognized by the National Institute of Mental Health, which in 1956 granted funds to the Massachusetts General Hospital Psychiatric Service to set up a Center for Community Studies. Dr. Marc Fried, a social psychologist, became the Research Coordinator.

A preliminary anthropological survey was carried out by Dr. Herbert Gans (1962). There emerged the image of a community that had preserved a peasant style of life and that for decades had operated as a port of entrance for immigrant families. Although they represented a mixture of Italian, Polish, Jewish, and Yankee origins, they had evolved a common pattern of life, with strong emphasis on kinship ties and mutual support throughout the neighborhood. Anything beyond the boundary of the West End was considered foreign territory. There was a disinclination to accept and value the style of life of the middle class. Peer groups with strong mutual loyalties and clearly defined leadership formed the matrix of daily life. Intellectual achievement was devalued. If persons had to leave, even as a consequence of upward social mobility, they would return frequently to the West End to demonstrate their loyalty and affection.

The helping agencies, including the hospital with its outpatient and inpatient services and the local settlement house, were regarded by the people as part of the same system of informal mutual obligations, in which the physician or social worker was viewed as a partner in a relationship of lasting personal loyalty, rather than in a limited, contractual arrangement for a specific kind of service. The recognition of this fact was useful in understanding how a doctor-patient relationship once established in the clinic seemed to lead to undesirable dependency reactions, the patient being unwilling to disengage himself from a particular doctor or health worker.

Anticipation, planning, and preparation for the renewal crisis were noticeably absent. It had been inconceivable to the inhabitants that an area which seemed highly livable to them and was provided with enviable recreational facilities should be defined by the decision-making bodies as an expendable slum and should, in fact, be destroyed. Only after the bulldozers arrived were there mass meetings and protest marches on City Hall. A long period of apathy and denial was then replaced by precipitous efforts to find new locations and clamors for assistance from the Relocation Authority or other agencies.

The imposed change of habitat was perceived as abandonment by the city government. It became clear that the population had lost the political leaders of two decades ago and had become less important as a voting group. Instead of relying on self-help and proper representation in the political arena, they had sought short-term help from professional agencies such as the Family Service, the settlement house, and the Massachusetts General Hospital. They had become quite dependent on these professional resources, and it became a major problem to transplant them and attach them to other resources in their new habitats.

Some leaders of social agencies also refused to believe in the reality of the renewal operation until a few weeks before the beginning of demolition, notwithstanding the continual publicity given to these plans in the media. Agencies, like individuals and families, were faced with the problem of finding a new location.

Because of their suspicion of strangers and readiness to expect exploitation, we were aware that access to a working-class population would be more likely to be feasible at a time of crisis. This proved to be the case. In the first phase of the study, a committee of agency leaders, including those in the Relocation Authority, welcomed the opportunity to meet with staff of the Psychiatry Service to review the plight of the large number of citizens who found the relocation a serious challenge to their adaptive resources. Thus, it was possible for us to become participant observers in the relocation process. The second phase was a systematic inquiry carried out by Dr. Fried and his associates, based on extensive survey-type interviews before and after relocation. The interviewers were initially received with the hope that they might be influential in stopping the renewal program.

A sample of approximately 500 families was studied in detail and provided data for a comprehensive study of the life-style in a working-class community (Fried 1973). Instead of the small middle-class family unit, which was assisted in the suburb by impersonal agencies (professional or commercial), we found a population in which emotional and material support was largely guaranteed by the complex bonds of large family and quasi-family groups. The fragmentation of these social networks caused by the relocation of individual households in a dispersed pattern throughout the whole metropolitan area brought about a great many grieflike reactions and a variety of pathological responses. Arrangements to facilitate the transition, including casework and financial assistance, turned out to be inadequate. Much effort was made to regain relationships after being scattered to different parts of the city. Groups of citizens would return from time to time to hang out on the street where their demolished houses used to be.

An additional source of survey data consisted of records of contacts with social and helath agencies before and after relocation. The population in the renewal area had harbored a number of persons with psychotic conditions, which were tolerated in the neighborhood and not defined as medical problems. In the process of transplantation, it was impossible to further accommodate them, and psychiatric help then became appropriate.

Postrelocation visits to the relocatees showed a large amount of discomfort, grieving, and lack of adaptation in their new homes. The persons most disturbed were those whose system of friends and kin was disrupted by the relocation. This was especially true for the elderly. Some people were delighted with the change, and many felt no sense of loss. "But for the majority, it seems quite precise to speak of their reactions as expressions of grief. These became manifest in the feelings of painful loss, the continued longing, the general depressive tone, frequent symptoms of psychological or somatic distress, the active work required in adapting to the altered situation, the sense of helplessness, the occasional expressions of both direct and displaced anger, and tendencies to idealize the lost place" (Fried 1963, p. 151).

Among two hundred and fifty women respondents, 26 percent reported that they still felt sad or depressed two years after the move; and another 20 percent reported a long period (six months to two years) of sadness or depression. Altogether, therefore, 46 percent gave evidence of a fairly severe grief reaction. The data showed only a slightly smaller percentage of the men (38 percent of 316) with long-term grief reactions. The true proportion of depressive reactions was undoubtedly higher, since many women and men who reported no feelings of sadness or depression indicated clearly depressive responses to other questions (Fried 1963).

The reorganization of daily role behaviors and routines required by transplantation into dissimilar metropolitan environments could also be accompanied by paranoid reactions along with depression. For example, a couple in their mid-thirties moved into a suburban neighborhood, where they now lived next door to a lieutenant colonel and his wife, with whom a social relationship would have been awkward. The woman missed her daily visit to the corner grocery store, where she used to meet her friends and exchange the news. As she did not drive the car, her husband now went and bought the food at a supermarket, thus depriving her of what she, with an Italian ethnic background, regarded as an essential part of her female role. In a state of idleness and depression, she began to fantasize about the women whom her husband might be meeting at the supermarket and became intensely jealous, without any insight into the psychological determinants of her distress.

In short, as Fried (1965) has expressed it:

Coping with the transition to a new social and residential experience, leaving a situation of embeddedness with a familiar and beloved place, undertaking a struggle with challenges which were not sought and which so often go beyond available psychological or social resources necessarily pose extremely difficult problems. The fact that less than one third of the entire sample was both satisfied and happy with the change indicates how small a proportion of the population of a working-class community is ready for this transition. Hypothetically, relocation can be conceived as an opportunity for change, for greater assimilation, for social mobility. However, the freedom to use these opportunities must first be achieved internally and become an aspect of the individual's adaptational potential."

City planners have been interested in our findings in connection with other programs for urban renewal. We emphasized to them that the West End population experienced itself as a target of administrative procedures without the opportunity for responsible participation in planning for their own future. Citizen participation was subsequently made a mandatory feature of federal relocation programs. But this is again a new role for people who have had no previous chance to practice it! Responsible participation cannot be demanded of people overnight but can be developed at a rather slow pace, with an initial period in which the display of distrust, anger, and depression must be expected and accepted. Meetings at which people shout and get angry with each other, such as we have witnessed on later occasions of urban renewal, may represent a salutory phase of communal growth, even though they alarm the public and put a severe strain on the political process.

As a mental health expert, one can hope to lessen the impact of crisis on large population groups if one impresses on the power structure the need for tolerating group emotional displays, which correspond to the early phase of grieving in individuals. This alone, however, cannot be sufficient unless other phases of coping behavior are encouraged: adequate sharing of information about the crisis, enough time to rehearse a variety of alternative solutions, and genuine community representation in the decision-making process.

There is also the question of how professional agencies can be of greatest help in such a crisis. We were impressed by the difficulty that a working-class population has, particularly when under stress, in making appropriate use of the different agencies and professions. A multiservice center—in which medical, legal, educational and job problems can be handled within one building, with arrangements for sharing information and collating the respective contributions of the different professional agents—is especially desirable under crisis conditions.

REFERENCES

Coelho, G.V., and Hamburg, D.A. (1963). Coping strategies in a new learning environment. *Archives of General Psychiatry* 9.

Chodoff, P.S., Friedman, S.B., and Hamburg, D.A. (1964). Stress, defenses and coping behavior observations in parents of children with malignant disease. *American Journal of Psychiatry* 120:743-749.

Eaton, J.W., ed. *Migration and Social Welfare Symposium.* New York: National Association of Social Workers.

Engel, G.L. (1961). Is grief a disease? *Psychosomatic Medicine* 23:18-22.

Fried, M. (1963). Grieving for a lost home. In *The Urban Condition,* ed. L.J. Duhl, pp. 151-171. New York: Basic Books.

——— (1965). Transitional functions of working-class communities. In *Mobility and Mental Health,* ed. M.B. Kantor. Springfield, Ill.: Charles C Thomas.

——— (1973). *The World of the Urban Working Class.* Cambridge: Harvard University Press.

Gans. H. (1962). *The Urban Villagers.* Glencoe, Illinois: Free Press.

Hamburg, D.A. (1953). Psychological adaptive processes in life-threatening injuries. Washington, D.C.: United States Government Printing Office.

Lewis, O. (1959). *Mexican Case Studies in the Culture of Poverty.* New York: Random House.

Murphy, J.M. (1965). *Migration and Mental Health.* New York: Milbank Memorial Fund.

Schmale, A.H. (1958). Relationship of separation and depression to disease. *Psychosomatic Medicine* 20:259-277.

Part III

Professional Roles in Mental Health

Introduction to Part III

Lindemann was constantly aware of the need to train a new generation of doctors and other health professionals who would relate what they were doing to the life situations of patients as well as to disease processes. Many who studied under him have testified that he was an inspiring teacher, whether he was interviewing a patient at "grand rounds" or expounding his ideas in a community mental health seminar. He also labored tirelessly on university committees at Harvard to ensure that concepts from the social sciences would be integrated into the Harvard Medical School curriculum. He encountered lively resistance from those who felt threatened by what Lindemann himself acknowledged as the blurring of the boundaries of medical practice. For example, one of his colleagues referred to him as a "glorified social worker"—an unintended compliment to a profession that historically has been concerned with the relevant human environment.

Chapter 9

Community Mental Health Training at the Massachusetts General Hospital

In this previously unpublished paper, Dr. Lindemann describes how, in taking charge of the Psychiatry Service, he became a change agent with Massachusetts General Hospital, transferring and teaching concepts and methods acquired in Wellesley to the hospital seen as a community. It does not deal in a comprehensive way with his administration, however, which included the inauguration of the Stanley Cobb laboratories for neurophysiological research, the planning of the new hundred-bed hospital, later named after him, in the Government Center, and the expansion of programs at the McLean Hospital. His insistence on viewing hospitals as only one link in the delivery system of health services was reinforced when Dr. John Knowles became Director of Massachusetts General Hospital in 1961. The congruence of their ideas led to a cordial relationship and was partly responsible for Dr. Lindemann's becoming chairman of the General Executive Committee in the last year of his stay.

The mental health program in the Harvard University Medical School came about when it was decided that medical students in the early stages of their development, as well as residents in psychiatry, should be confronted with some of the concerns and methods of public health. Returning to the Harvard Medical School from the School of Public Health in July, 1954, I attempted to find the most suitable mental health orientation for a psychiatric team in a general hospital, one to which residents and other trainees could be introduced. This resulted in a new educational emphasis, whereby the curative preoccupation of the budding physician would hopefully be expanded to a commitment to be the guardian of the health of a population and to be cognizant of mental health issues facing segments of that population.

The implementation of this program was greatly aided by the continuing technical studies and methodological advances carried out under the direction of Dr. Gerald Caplan at the Harvard School of Public Health. His appointment to the Medical School faculty and to the staff of my department at the Masschusetts General Hospital, and my continued faculty membership in Public Health, ensured close collaboration, which was beneficial to both areas.

An early expression of the altered orientation in the Medical School was the course in growth and development, which incorporated some aspects of the previous offering in psychiatry. This two-year course for first- and second-year students was taught by representatives of several disciplines in addition to child and adult psychiatry: the biostatistician from the Department of Preventive Medicine, those in the Anatomy Department concerned with embryology and developmental anatomy, and mental health specialists, including psychologists and other social scientists. The mental health faculty introduced the students to a range of social-psychological material, beginning with personality structure and responses to typical stresses in the life cycle and extending to the structure and dynamics of the family and of other institutions and social organizations. The students, therefore, were encouraged to view individual health and illness in relation to the ways in which groupings in the social environment color the pathway of a given life cycle and affect the relative physical, social and emotional well-being of a population.

The first year of the course considered the material from the standpoint of positive health; in the second year, pathological issues were brought into focus. Student reaction was favorable, and the level of interest in broad cultural problems seemed surprisingly high to those who had imagined that medical students as a group were primarily biologically oriented and basically disinterested in the social sciences. However, this course proved to be too eclectic for several members of the sponsoring faculty committee and was replaced after several years by a course entitled, The Study of Human Behavior.

At the more advanced level of the residency in psychiatry, it was necessary to evolve a set of mental health operations in the general hospital to which residents could be introduced as part and parcel of their basic specialty training, with the encouragement and careful guidance of senior staff; hence, we formed the Mental Health Service within the Psychiatric Service. A pattern emerged on principles that were already quite familiar, since they were similar to those previously applied in our community work outside the hospital. The major objective underlying this program can be stated in the form of a question: Can health considerations be added to the medical objectives of the hospital in such a way that the medical staff member will view himself as a health officer?

The psychiatrist member of the mental health team is usually the one called on initially for consultation regarding a given problem patient. Through his approach to the problem, his questions and comments, he attempts to suggest that the relationship of the patient to the ward population and its caretakers is worthy of the joint attention of himself and the medical staff. Having been helpful in a given case, the mental health representative hopes to interest the staff in the emotional well-being of the total patient population of the medical or surgical ward, including those who are allegedly mentally healthy as well as those with special needs in the personality sphere.

One such area of special needs came to our attention from the orthopedic ward. It involved the effect of protracted passivity in a cast for those personality types for whom a higher rate of activity is a necessary prerequisite for maintaining their mental health. The challenge for the orthopedic staff and mental health team is to find a means of screening patients at the very beginning of ward residence, in order to assess their personality requirements, rather than waiting for the ward experience to produce casualties.

Thus, the mental health team seeks to study the emotional hazards as well as the supportive features of the ward experience of the patient, in order ultimately to help create the healthiest possible emotional environment for all patients. Borrowing a phrase from the educators, with whom we had worked closely in the community, we invited the medical staff to examine the ward "curriculum." Ward curricula, while in harmony with medical considerations, often relate largely to staff rather than to patient needs; they may sometimes conflict with the latter's emotional requirements. A basic principle of our work emphasizes that a given state of affairs is almost always maintained by a set of forces that must be understood and altered before constructive and lasting changes can be effected. Consequently, our consultants broadened their focus to include a concern for the mental health of the staff as well as the patients.

Those who work in hospitals know that the social process of a ward is likely to involve typical patterns of stress. These patterns are derived from a number of factors, such as the emotional impact of illness and death, the universal ambivalence about nurturance and dependence, shifts in role functions emanating from changes within a profession or from edicts passed down from the hierarchy, and conflicting value orientations and expectations within a complex organization. Hospital staff groups, having to live in continuous proximity and to function at a generally high level of task efficiency, appear prone to develop protective devices against disruption by ever-present stresses. Among such protective reactions are barriers to communication, carefully guarded lines of authority and of the right to initiate activities, and well-defended functional domains. Because they serve a defensive function, these arrangements are not easily altered, even though they seem at times to react adversely upon the emotional well-being of patients.

Viewed from the patient's perspective, he is at the mercy of the system and plays a passive role within it. From the staff's viewpoint, the patient's passivity may be felt to be an asset, contributing to ward tranquillity and to his own recovery, not to mention the peace of mind of those responsible for his care. From a strictly medical and surgical point of view, the less known about the patient's emotional response to his situation, the better.

The mental health officer must be prepared to stand by those hospital staff groups that begin to confront and alter defensive ward patterns. He is helped in this effort by the fact that many staff members themselves are troubled by some of the inappropriate protective arrangements. Awareness of the interplay of forces is not restricted to the mental health team and its social science allies. Recognition that all is not as efficiently tranquil as it appears may be heightened by the fact that a few doctors, nurses, and other personnel become casualties as they attempt to live and work within these pressures. Attention to the maintenance and enhancement of the emotional well-being of the staff as part of the social environment of the patient population is a continuous function of the Mental Health Service.

Some of the most complex considerations relating to hospital process have come to the fore in the area of rehabilitation. Experiences with a newly developed ward for rehabilitation purposes may serve as an example of the kinds of forces one encounters when one enters the situation as a mental health worker and the orientation one adopts in order to be effective.

The services of the rehabilitation unit are largely educational in nature. Role confusion results as the ward population begins to perceive itself more and more as students, though from the hospital standpoint it remains a patient population. Furthermore, these individuals are being treated, ministered to, and trained by a team of people, thereby compounding the role problem because of the team's special makeup. These professions—the physical therapist, social worker, nurse, and orthopedic doctor—find it difficult to operate with each other. Resulting tension systems appear to resemble those reported by Stanton and Schwartz (1954) in their studies in the mental hospital, where patients were likely to grow worse as a result of disagreement between professional groups.

After preliminary contacts with the chief of service and other staff members regarding individual patients, the general nature of some of the living problems seemed clear. The director of the program then became interested in the formation of a mental health team whose purpose would be to review with staff members the flow of social events on the ward and to help formulate plans for dealing with the more stressful features. The mental health team in this instance consisted of a psychiatrist, a psychologist, and a social anthropologist, with Mental Health Fellows taking over parts of the work under supervision. Observations focused particularly on the effects on the ward and its role relationships of the inclusion of the physical therapists in the caretaking group. The respective status of the several professions as self-perceived and as ascribed by others was especially significant. The physical therapists supplant the nurses as the major profession in the ward in terms of their effectiveness with patients' physical problems. As a result, they cannot defer to the nurse, even though she, by hospital tradition, is in charge of the day-to-day life of the ward. While continuing to bear primary responsibility for ward events, the nurse finds her corresponding authority and prestige challenged. Her relationships with patients, who are now quasi-students, become less authoritative. Consequent clashes over status—for example, who can give orders—are almost inevitable.

In regular meetings with the several groups it was possible to review what was actually going on, basing this assessment on an altered perspective, including consideration of role, status, and ward-system factors. There was perceptible movement toward new kinds of professional self-perceptions. It remained an opportunity for further research to find out how these alterations affected the patients' physical and emotional health, not to mention the happiness and effectiveness of the caretakers themselves.

Rather than being concerned only with a given patient who needs the ministrations of a skilled psychiatrist or with a given social unit that needs the insights afforded by social and interpersonal analysis, the Mental Health Service seeks to review the flow or frequency of different kinds of psychological casualties occurring in various sections of the hospital community. The application of field-epidemiological techniques will lead in certain instances to clear-cut actions designed to reduce a particular form of aberrant reaction. One example of the success of such an application involved the Eye and Ear Infirmary, where changing from a double-patch to a single-patch technique reduced the frequency of occurrence of confusional states. The importance of relating mental health operations to laboratory research is indicated by the fact that our service was alert to recent psychological research concerning the effects of sensory deprivation and was able to apply this knowledge to the postoperative cataract patient's problem.

This is only one example from a hospital context, where many medical procedures may carry with them features hazardous for mental health. It is possible to identify such hazards on a population-wide basis and to try to achieve policy alterations consistent with medical prudence.

The special arrangements of each hospital must differ, depending on the prevailing culture patterns. Each psychiatry department will naturally tend to form special relationships with other departments, and each psychiatrist will develop his own lines of communication to other individuals. What is important is to work toward a gradually increasing understanding of the social forces that compel members of the other departments to defend the arrangements and routines they have worked out. Just as in psychotherapy, where we know that a patient will not surrender his defenses until he has found a more promising alternate solution for his problems, the medical man or surgeon will insist on his concepts and his routines until we have found with him plans that work better for him and his patients alike.

So far, I have reviewed some of the preoccupations of the Mental Health Service with intrahospital events. The hospital itself is embedded in a larger community, represented by its outpatients and by the population within the residential area surrounding it. The Mental Health Service was concerned with both these groups.

Through the active collaboration of the chief of the medical outpatient service, the Mental Health Service staff was able to witness the flow of the patient population through this service.

In addition to consultations regarding some of the more emotionally disturbed individuals, who were sometimes referred for psychiatric help, other matters caught our attention. For example, one problem of the medical team was the excessive dependency of certain patients, who develop an exaggerated need for continued contact with the physician or social worker with whom an initial relationship has been made. The wish for contact continues, even though the need for the clinic no longer exists from a medical standpoint. Some physicians develop an entourage of such patients. They complain about the patients' dependence, while at the same time seeming, in some fashion, to contribute to it. From the mental health point of view, this social pattern is fostered unwittingly by certain techniques of the internist and surgeon. Under some circumstances, it may hinder the flow of patients toward other more appropriate caretaking resources within the community, or it may restrict the patient's efforts at finding more suitable nurturant figures. Consultation with the staff of the outpatient service attempted to make explicit the less apparent features of the problem in order to resolve the dependency and direct the patients to more suitable helping agents.

One area in which a crisis approach turned out to be relevant was the emergency ward. In the last ten years at our hospital, emergency ward patients have doubled in number—to about 44,000 from about 22,000; however, the number of psychiatric patients has increased tenfold—to 3,000 a year from 300— requiring a considerable increase in psychiatric staff. This came about when we stopped limiting ourselves to looking for mental disease and began to appraise health needs and unsolved life crises. The life crises in which these patients seek help are the kinds of predicaments we encountered both in Wellesley and in the West End: the loss of another person, a bereavement response, a transition problem.

A life-crisis approach also led to increased success with

alcoholics, an important component of the emergency ward population. Our staff psychiatrist, Dr. Morris Chafetz, was able to demonstrate that the initial contact with a skilled person makes an important difference for the subsequent behavior of the alcoholic. Shortly after the opening of our alcohol clinic, the percentage of alcoholics who would accept an emergency ward referral to the clinic for psychiatric assistance was less than one percent. Apparently, something happened in the conversation during the initial examination that contributed to a decision against returning. Often this meeting took place with the patient in a state of intoxication, which rendered him temporarily incompetent; or a somatic illness as a sequel or complication of drinking required diagnosis and treatment. The drinking, the addictive behavior itself, did not become the object of the examination or treatment.

Just as frequently happens with attempted suicide, the secondary phenomena were studied, but the endangering psychological condition seemed medically uninteresting. Only when it became a general rule that all such patients were to be examined in the emergency ward not only by the general medical man but also by the psychiatrist was it possible to define the condition of the addict as a life crisis, existing alongside of the somatic symptoms; to show interest in this crisis; and to offer the patient the prospect of further help if he would come to the clinic. The result of this administrative change was quite dramatic: In the ensuing three years, nine out of every ten alcoholics referred to the alcohol clinic for psychiatric assistance accepted the referral. It was then possible, by studying this large group of patients, to describe the life problems that addicted persons are unable to master without recourse to intoxication.

Another phase of the Mental Health Service program involved the assignment of staff and Fellows to the West End research described in chapter 8. Graduate students from the Department of Social Relations at Harvard were also included. The study of a relocated working-class population became a significant training opportunity for individuals in both the social and medical sciences. The former were confronted with issues of medical practice, which could further enrich their experimental and conceptual knowledge, whereas the latter were challenged to confront social and cultural issues and to examine with greater sophistication the social environments from which patients in the medical outpatient service and other hospital services come.

As the pattern of a hospital mental health service unfolds, its multifaceted nature becomes apparent. It continues to offer direct help with psychiatrically disturbed patients as before. It moves out increasingly into the flow of life in the hospital, relating as it can to significant segments of this community. Yet it recognizes that as part of the hospital community itself, it is often perceived as having vested interests of its own, including values that may clash with those of others and strivings for satisfactions and rewards that do not always exist in abundance for all those who seek them. Therefore, it moves toward the development of independent and autonomous activities, which may represent a secure base of operations from which workers can go forth with some security in their efforts to work cooperatively with others.

Most important, the hospital mental health service finds stimulation and security in the development of a coherent frame of reference, whereby the following may be facilitated: (1) The hospital moves into focus as a community with its several segments, a hierarchy of dominant values, typical reactions to major stresses, and favored modes of work. (2) Staff groups move into focus as caretakers whose methods of handling medical concerns and intrastaff relationships affect groups of patients. (3) The patient population moves into focus as a component of the community, composed of sub-groupings according to socioeconomic characteristics, the specific nature of the medical problem and its consequent emotional hazards, and personality predispositions, which render some individuals more vulnerable than others to special sets of circumstances encountered in the course of their treatment.

REFERENCES

Stanton, A., and Schwartz, M.S., (1954). *The Mental Hospital.* New York: Basic Books.

Chapter 10

Preventive Intervention in Situational Crises

The original purpose of this paper contained in chapter 10, which was presented at a Congress of Applied Psychology in Copenhagen in 1961, was to suggest ways in which psychologists might participate in an effort to reduce rates of mental illness. It recapitulates Dr. Lindemann's thinking about prevention. Beginning with the bereavement observations, he showed how these were extended to other kinds of crises and were then pursued in community settings as well as in the hospital, using collaboration with other professions as a vehicle for intervention. The paper concludes by enumerating the functions that the psychologist as mental health worker may be able to fulfill.

Dr. Lindemann considered this one of his best papers. In 1964 he modified it slightly to apply to psychiatrists rather than to psychologists, and he gave it in the new form at the Sixth International Congress of Psychotherapy in London in 1965, under the title, "The Timing of Psychotherapy." That he could assign the same mental health role to practitioners of two different disciplines points to his belief in a generic role for mental health personnel, as well as recalling that he himself was originally trained and worked as a psychologist.

Preventive efforts in the field of mental disease have barely begun to show fruit. The early use of penicillin has prevented almost all cases of general cerebral paresis. The control of the use of poisons in industrial manufacturing has done away with psychosis such as the "mad hatters." Early intervention in enzyme deficiency, such as the metabolic error involved in the formation of phenylperuvic acid, has helped to reduce the development of mental retardation. However, the control of those factors that might lead to neuroses or psychoses on the basis of traumatic early experiences or because of the absence of needed environmental factors at critical periods of personality development is still in its infancy. This is not surprising because personality theory is still a most controversial field, and studies up to now have not been possible on a scale and at a level of complexity that would be required to establish conclusive evidence for the linkage between noxious event and subsequent pathology.

It seemed to us that we might make headway if we could free ourselves from the limitations of inquiry imposed by the traditional methods of clinical diagnosis in terms of disease entities such as neuroses and psychoses. We questioned the implicit assumption that emotional disorders are confined within specific individuals. A way had to be found to include the interpersonal component and the mutuality of responses within social systems involved in emotional disorders. We therefore looked or tried to find events representing a change in interpersonal relations that might possibly lead to disease. An opportunity for such observations offered itself at the time of a disaster in Boston—a fire in The Coconut Grove nightclub, which brought many severely burned persons to the hospital.

The surgeons called for psychological and psychiatric assistance because many patients did not cooperate with the procedures. It soon became obvious that uncertainty about the fate of other members of the family and grief about their loss presented a serious obstacle to the patients' successful convalescence from their injuries.

Studies on bereavement and grief reactions provide a model for the approach to emotional disturbances that may be precursors of true mental disease or at least may represent medically important variations in emotional well being and adjustments. Whenever one raises questions of mental health rather than of mental illness, and whenever one is concerned with communitywide measures for prevention of illness, one has the task of learning to discriminate the benign from the danger signals. Freud (1917) himself distinguished the benign patterns of mourning from the malignant features of melancholia. Our own earlier studies in bereavement were concerned with the problem of grief as a psychogenic determinant of ulcerative colitis and as an obstacle to proper recovery of burn victims from their injuries. Since then, a considerable body of information has been accumulated on grief and separation reactions by Bowlby (1958, 1961) and Spitz (1958), with emphasis on children, whereas Engel (1953, 1961) and Schmale (1958) studied the relationship of grief to somatic illness in a broader frame of reference, and Barry (1954) traced statistically the relationship of parental loss at specified ages to subsequent illness.

I will proceed here to paraphrase the essential components of the process of grieving, to specify the physiological, psychological, and social system factors that seem related to the severity and possible failure of the process of mourning, and to show the various ways in which such information has been used as a basis for certain forms of preventive intervention in a variety of life situations that might lead to emotional disease.

Systematic interviews with a variety of acutely bereaved

persons between the ages of twelve and sixty made it possible to circumscribe the syndrome of grieving and to compare those processes found in *self-limited* forms of such conditions with other forms which are *maladaptive,* and which develop into conditions indistinguishable from disease. We had reason to conclude that many of these reactions, whether psychosomatic, psychoneurotic, or psychotic, were substitutes for normal grieving and did not come to resolution because the essentials of grief work did not take place.

After every severe bereavement, which means after separation from and after cessation of interaction with an emotionally relevant other person that is not expected to be restored, there normally ensues a syndrome of psychological disturbances (heightened preoccupation with the image of the deceased, painful preoccupation with the emotional state of sorrow); physiological disturbances (loss of appetite, excessive fatigue, respiratory abnormalities), and disturbances in social relations (excessive hostility to others, helplessness, inability to interact effectively). This syndrome, fluctuating in intensity, will gradually become more tolerable and will finally disappear. The mastery of this abnormal state is achieved by *grief work,* which has three significant components: (1) the acceptance of the painful emotions involved, (2) the active review of a variety of experiences and events shared with the lost person, and (3) the gradual rehearsal and testing of new patterns of interaction and role relationships that can replace some of the functions the deceased fulfilled in the survivor's life.

In other words, the original state of confusion and perplexity following a loss is replaced by the process of grief work, in which a person accepts and masters the experience of sorrow, in a systematic way reviews his past associations with the deceased, and then raises the question, "And what will I do now?" We contrasted this self-limited grief reaction with the types of grieving found in patients suffering from a variety of medical illnesses.

Ulcerative colitis turned out to be a form of psychosomatic illness that frequently follows an unsuccessful attempt at grieving. Other patients developed conditions resembling a psychoneurosis—going from doctor to doctor to ask for help with symptoms reenacted from the last illness of the person who died and receiving the label of *hypochondriasis*. Another form of illness can be misdiagnosed as schizophrenia, in that the ego-identity of the survivor becomes blended with the ego of the deceased person. The survivor begins to act like the deceased, or he begins to feel that he is two persons.

We finally encounter a characteristic feature of all states of abnormal grief: Abnormal grievers seem to have difficulty in recalling the image of the deceased; they are troubled with excessive hostility; and they often make unwise life decisions, such as moving away, alienating their friends, or locking up the belongings of the deceased. In other words, we have a series of well-adaptive and of maladaptive responses to a specific social event—the cessation of interaction with an emotionally relevant other person.

The condition of ulcerative colitis became a very important one in which to study the effect of psychological intervention, because diarrhea is such a sensitive indicator of the fluctuations in the severity of the condition. It became clear that there were two main approaches: (1) the traditional approach of the psychiatrist, who confronts the patient with his loss and helps him to grieve; and (2) what has been called *role-taking therapy*, in which the therapist utilizes the great readiness of the mourner to transfer to him the characteristic features of the deceased. In this second approach, the doctor acts as though he were the deceased person and, temporarily during the emergency period of the illness, maintains a relationship resembling the lost role relationship.

Bereavement conditions may follow immediately after the loss, or they may be delayed. For example, a young girl who was placed with her siblings in an orphanage when her mother disappeared had no visible reaction at the time, but she developed severe anxiety and bloody diarrhea four years later when she learned that her mother had not died, as she had supposed, but had actually deserted the family. At the time of the onset of illness, she had just been placed as a working girl in a new family. Instead of attempting to treat her with psychotherapy, it was decided to try to reconstitute the original family by reuniting her with her father and brothers. This was done successfully, and there has been no relapse for fifteen years.

Although the somatic conditions are seen in a general hospital, there are psychological reactions that may be studied in guidance clinics. A young boy of fourteen loses his father and is brought to the clinic by his mother because she cannot make him mind. He is found to have unconsciously incorporated the image of his father and now assumes all the father's prerogatives, including the right to dominate his mother. A girl who loses her father may begin to show masculine behavior. If a mother loses a small child, the *incorporation mechanism* may operate to make the mother appear as helpless as the child was and show excessive dependency on other persons. It is important to realize that in such cases where the image of the deceased is incorporated, the person has no awareness of the change that has taken place in his own behavior.

Ambivalence or hostile dependence in the lost relationship can lead to just as severe a pathological mourning reaction as love. Multiple losses obviously complicate the grief work. A delayed reaction to an unresolved previous crisis may be reactivated by a subsequent crisis and thereby constitutes multiple bereavement.

We see, then, that a change in a social system—namely, cessation of interaction—may be followed either by a process of healthy reorganization of psychological and physiological functioning or by an abnormal state in which the resolution of a crisis does not take place. To understand the full meaning of this crisis, we explored the concept of *role* as it is used in social science. The word *role* refers to the activities and to the behavior the role partner is justified in expecting from the other person. Complementary activities are going on continuously in groups and between individuals. Bereavement constitutes an interruption of a profile of mutual role behavior. The replacement of specific roles is the peculiar problem of grieving. If almost all role activities are taking place in a one-to-one relationship, the loss will be particularly severe. This we have seen in persons who have nursed someone through a long terminal illness. The typical role relationship in ulcerative colitis is the exclusive, obligatory relationship.

How will a mental health worker witnessing the response to bereavement intervene in the most effective way? He must realize that there is a time issue involved. There is usually an initial state of perplexity in which the person is not very accessible; following this, both he and the mourner must expect an expression of emotion of the first magnitude, involving grief. Within the puritan tradition, there is little tolerance for such emotional expression. The war widow is not supposed to show mourning; the youngster who loses all his friends when the family moves is not supposed to show any effect of this; and if a governess who was loved by a child has to leave, the mother, instead of accepting the child's mourning, will demand that all the love be transferred to her. Thus, the first mental health considerations have to do with giving the person permission to feel suffering and to express it.

The next stage has to do with the organization of grief work. Here the difficulty is the magnitude of the task, which is approached first in a global way, with the wish to have the person back. Grief work means to tackle this problem step by step, by reviewing the formerly shared activities and experiences and searching for possibilities of allocating some aspects of these interactions to new role partners. This process can be learned and taught in therapy, but the therapist himself must have had an opportunity to acquire the necessary techniques. He must also know when to try to postpone the necessity for grieving when it would be dangerous to the person, through suitable role-taking.

It is obvious that grieving for a person who has died is only one situation in which a pattern of reaction to loss is activated. In a general hospital, one finds results of separation from parts of one's own body: In surgery, the loss of an eye, a leg, or a womb lead to genuine mourning reactions.

One may also look at grieving as a particular form of *role transition*, as the limiting case of having to redesign role functions on a major scale. Transitions in life from one role state to another, and separations or replacement of certain persons by other persons happen all the time. Some people make these transitions well; others have tremendous difficulties. Out of these considerations a whole series of studies developed focused on forms of reaction to role transition in the community.

On the other hand, we may consider that what we have said about grief work might also apply to the psychological work called forth by the *anticipation of a threatening situation*. The rehearsal of future action necessitated by anxiety-arousing events appears to show features quite similar to those of grief work—namely, the anticipatory review of interactional events with the right timing and whittling down the problem ahead to manageable proportions, attended by an amount of anxiety that can be handled without a sense of paralysis or despair. For both anticipatory threats and retrospective losses, then, the mastery of attending emotions, the review of possible suitable responses, and the rehearsal of feasible role patterns are the ingredients of the necessary psychological work, which provides an opportunity for assistance.

These *situational responses* constitute *crises* in vulnerable individuals for whom the mobilization of new resources and the demand for a new organization of their role functions threaten disintegration or the use of pathological defenses. We are distinguishing this type of crisis from the so-called developmental crises of adolescence and pregnancy described by Erikson (1959) and Bibring (1959), respectively. Caplan (1961) elaborated on the details of crisis behavior at the occasion of a premature birth. Goodrich (1961) studied the critical period of adaptation of newly-wedded couples, and Hamburg applied a similar type of thinking to the adaptive problems of foreign students in the process of acculturation.

Many opportunities for *preventive intervention* become apparent when the concept of role transition is extended from the crisis of bereavement to other kinds of changes imposed by the stage of the life cycle. We were able to gain access to the population of Wellesley, a Boston suburb, where we opened a mental health agency and obtained the cooperation of the citizens to let us study the way in which they met particular transitions, such as the children's entry into kindergarten or preparation for the profession of nursing. We learned that there is a spectrum of responses, not only for the child but also for his family, to kindergarten entry that includes some pathological responses—such as parental regression, in which the mother communicates her anxiety at being back in a schoolroom to the child, or jealousy of the child's relationship to the teacher. A good many school phobias of children are related to crisis behavior on the part of the mother, who cannot tolerate the role transition involved in that particular social system.

We were asked by a hospital school of nursing to find out why it, like many nursing schools, was having a dropout rate of thirty to forty percent. We applied the crisis concept of role transition. Dr. Pearl Rosenberg, a psychologist, met with groups of first-year nursing students to study with them the role implications of becoming a student nurse (Rosenberg and Fuller 1957). A good many of them were mildly disturbed about three problems: (1) the close intimacy with each other required by the program of instruction, which calls for them to practice nursing procedures on each other; (2) the disillusionment with the "Lady in White," who represents their ideal self-image but who turns out to be all too human; and (3) the problem of not being able to tolerate the celibacy that is part of the role definition of the nurse, at least during the training period. A review in the groups of these crisis components brought about a dramatic reduction in the dropout rate of student nurses at the nursing school: Everyone wanted to stay, even some whom the school wanted to be rid of. Just as helping a griever to grieve too well may make his behavior incompatible with the prescriptions of society, if you salvage the whole class, it may clash with the expectation of the institution.

We began, then, to look at the general hospital as a context for role transition. The whole patient population, rather than a few patients with psychiatric disorders, became our focus as a *population at risk,* exposed to certain psychological hazards and social customs. As soon as we formulated this, we became interested in surgery. We used to have for many years a high rate of referrals from the Eye and Ear Service of people who had had cataract operations. These patients became confused, depressed, disoriented, and were sent to our ward when the Eye and Ear Infirmary was unable to handle them. These patients got over this condition fairly rapidly, but there was an aftermath of bewilderment on the part of their families as to why this had happened.

Viewing the eye operation as a crisis accompanying certain role expectations about future functioning on the part of the patients, we realized that instead of being allowed to *see* after the operation, they would be blindfolded on both eyes, to keep the eyes from moving. Patients were not prepared for this enforced blindness, which seemed to them to indicate that the operation had failed. Furthermore, lacking visual cues for interaction with people, they were exposed to a succession of strange nurses, instead of being supported through the experience by one nurse with whom they could have continuous contact. Our crisis intervention in this instance was the simple one of analyzing the transition through the surgery from one role profile to another and making it possible to mobilize environmental preventive resources. This type of psychosis had altogether disappeared from the hospital.

It is perhaps useful to think of the field of prevention as being many little things, and not to think that one has to begin right away by conquering schizophrenia. The psychologist can make use of the crisis concept in the general hospital insofar as he studies the psychosocial situation present in all forms of illness. In our hospital, psychologists work in the emergency ward together with the surgeons in order to study the large segment of patients, sometimes as many as eighty percent, who arrive there primarily because of an emotional crisis even though their presenting complaint is of a physical nature. This has been recognized as significant improvement of the ward and its efficiency, because previously the patients who were sent away after physical examination without attention to the basic emotional problem kept returning over and over again.

And so in trying both in a general hospital and in a community agency to be population oriented and to use crises as legitimate targets for study just as physicians study diseases, we have come to believe that our range of activities for the psychologist has greatly expanded. On the medical and surgical wards, the traditional referral of patients for the diagnosis of a mental disorder has been augmented by a large number of requests for consultations with the psychologists and psychiatrists for the study of emotional crises. Many of these problems involve not only the patients but also the caretaking personnel and their emotional responses to a particular patient. Furthermore, the agency for preventive work, which the hospital has developed in Wellesley and which is directed by a psychologist, finds a rapidly increasing demand for its services in crisis consultation. We might say then that this way of formulating problems and issues, added to the traditional clinical approach, has two effects: (1) to stimulate and enable studies in areas where otherwise one would not look; and (2) to make it possible, even with limited information, to intercede in a helpful or protective manner where otherwise the population would go without help.

The general hospital of the future will be a center for the maintenance of health in addition to being a resource for the cure of disease and the rehabilitation of the disabled. The role expectations concerning the psychological professions in this new context are quite different from the traditional view of the clinical psychologist. The target for his research and his service are not sick individuals but an aggregate of people who all face a hazardous situation with respect to their health. The people so endangered do not reach out for help. On the contrary, they often resent intervention and even inquiry. The gratitude and appreciation expected from one's patients is not likely to be visible because the goal of the preventive effort is a reduction in the occurrence or rate of disease rather than the cure of an established malady. This change in focus is not at all easy for young psychiatrists. Perhaps it will be achieved with less stress by psychologists.

At any rate, it is necessary to have certain skills of motivating people to cooperate, whether in research or in a program of prevention. Many segments of the population that one would like to study are accessible via members of other professions whom we have designated the caretaking professions in the community. The most important of these professions—namely, the educators, the clergy, the law professions, and the social services—each have a tradition concerning the segment of the population and the kind of problems that they consider their own. The basic attributes of the role they play vis-à-vis their clients, the style of their procedures, the values determining their decisions, and the body of information they teach in their professional schools show profound differences. Yet in many problems of prevention, cooperative endeavors are involved.

Returning for a moment to our studies of bereavement, we see immediately that the state of grief is not recognized as a disease but is accepted only as a possible precursor of disease, that the treatment of grief is traditionally not the task of the psychiatrist or psychologist but of the clergyman, and that different societies and different religious groups within these societies have developed culturally sanctioned prescriptions for the management of grief. Any preventive measures that may be tested and suggested for general acceptance may clash with valued traditions of procedure.

That this problem does not only exist with respect to psychological habits is obvious when we consider the tremendous resistance aroused at the time of the vaccination against smallpox and the persistent efforts to block general acceptance of the fluoridation of water to prevent tooth decay, not to mention the great difficulties encountered in trying to change food habits and sanitation conditions in developing countries.

All this requires not only cooperative interprofessional endeavor but also pooling of information and skills between various disciplines, notably the social sciences and psychology. We believe that in all those efforts dealing with the psychological component of preventive work the psychologist might well take the leadership of preventive agencies or mental health centers. In this role he will be the coordinator of a program in which he may use the psychiatrist as consultant for the diagnosis of emotional disorders and as a source of referral for treatment of established disease. However, it will be he who endeavors to allocate conditions of emotional disturbance to various community resources and to develop channels of communication with key persons and institutions in the community. It is he who in churches and schools and social agencies and correctional institutions will combine his judgment with that of the other professions in identifying hazardous situations and forestalling dangerous consequences.

The line between social deviance as culpable behavior on the one hand and as excusable sickness on the other has proved uncertain. It seems to be redrawn by each new generation, and it differs from society to society and from class to class. The legal attitude in different countries regarding alcoholism, homosexuality, and suicide are obvious examples. The psychologist, as mental health worker in the community, will therefore be involved at many levels and exposed to many problems of social structure and social process. There are, however, at least four functions requiring teachable skills:

1. The psychologist may follow the model of crisis intervention as used in bereavement situations. He will survey the population involved, identify endangered individuals, and suggest protective measures.

2. He will serve as mental health consultant to other professional individuals whose job it is, or who choose, to deal with population in crisis. The clergyman facing problems of role transition in his church, the teacher facing classroom problems, and the health officer in the wake of a disaster will turn to the psychologist for clarification of hazards and for the significance of their own involvement and their own emotions in facing the crisis. We have found it useful to designate the variety of professional persons who are likely to be involved with families and neighborhoods at the time of crisis as *caretaking professions*. No matter how different their goals and value orientations, it is possible to share with them concerns about the hazardous component of emotional crises and the

timing and direction of steps that can be taken within the framework of their respective professions to help prevent serious consequences. Caplan (1964) has elaborated the technical detail of this type of assistance, which we speak of as crisis consultation.

3. The psychologist will be a resource person for city planners and public servants, who have the responsibility for making decisions involving the emotional well-being of segments of the population. An example is forced migration of population, which frequently occurs not only as a consequence of war but also in peacetime as part of the renewal of metropolitan centers. The forced relocation of the population in the neighborhood of our hospital, the West End of Boston, has provided an opportunity to study in detail the mental health hazards inherent in this event and to provide information that can be used for future planned relocations of this sort. Weinberg has studied the adaptive consequences of immigration to the new state of Israel.

4. The most important function will remain that of research. The clinical psychologist has always been primarily a scholar. His work with cases of brain damage and his participation in psychotherapy and pharmacotherapy have always served to advance theory and to place clinical practice solidly on a basis of established proof rather than intuition and tradition. In public health work and preventive medicine, he will have a vastly expanded region of research problems and opportunities for upholding the scientific approach. For the last decade, the Psychiatric Service at the Massachusetts General Hospital, in cooperation with the Harvard School of Public Health, has endeavored to make a community mental health agency in a middle-class suburb and a center for community studies in a working-class area gathering places of psychologists and other social scientists, together with medical investigators who are all interested in the study of adaptive behavior for graduate and

postdoctoral training for psychologists in preventive community work. Of course, our own work represents only a small part of a rapidly increasing involvement of psychologists in teams concerned with prevention.

REFERENCES

Barry, H. (1954). Critical ages for parental death in psychoneurosis. *Journal of Nervous and Mental Diseases* 120:401.

Bibring, G.L. (1959). Some considerations of the psychological processes in pregnancy. *Psychoanalytic Study of the Child* 14:113-121.

Bowlby, J. (1958). The nature of the child's tie to his mother. *International Journal of Psycho-Analysis* 39:350-373.

——— (1961). Processes of mourning. *International Journal of Psycho-Analysis* 42:317-340.

Caplan, G., ed. (1961). *Prevention of Mental Disorders in Children*. New York: Basic Books.

Caplan, G. (1964). *Principles of Preventive Psychiatry*. New York: Basic Books.

Engel, G.L. (1953). Homeostasis, behavioral adjustment and the concept of health and disease. In *Mid-Century Psychiatry*, ed. R. Grinker, pp. 33-59. Springfield, Illinois: Charles Thomas.

——— (1961). Is grief a disease? *Psychosomatic Medicine* 23:18-22.

Erikson, E. (1959). *Identity and the Life Cycle*. New York: International Universities Press.

Freud, S. (1917). Mourning and melancholia. *Standard Edition* 14:243-258.

Goodrich, D.W. (1961). Possibilities for preventive intervention during initial personality formation. In *Prevention of Mental Disorders in Children*, ed. G. Caplan. New York: Basic Books.

Hamburg, D. Plasma and urinary corticosteroid levels in naturally occuring psychological stresses. In *Ultra Structure and Metabolism of the Nervous System,* ed. S. Korey. *Ass. res. nerv. ment. dis.* Monograph series.

Rosenberg, P., and Fuller, M. (1957). Dynamic analysis of the student nurse. *Group Psychotherapy* 10:22-37.

Schmale, A.H. (1958). Relationship of separation and depression to disease. *Psychosomatic Medicine* 20:259-277.

Spitz, R.A. (1958). On the genesis of superego components. *Psychoanalytic Study of the Child* 13:375-404.

Part IV

Addressing Change

Introduction to Part IV

The idea in the following chapters is profoundly simple: Confronted with changes of a certain magnitude, people, both as individuals and as members of social networks, experience predictable feelings of bewilderment and loss and engage in typical sequences of behavior in efforts at adaptation. Successful grieving becomes the paradigm for successful coping with any sort of change. The frequency with which such coping miscarries, particularly on the level of institutions, justifies the training and deployment of *social therapists*.

Lindemann examines a variety of situations in order to illustrate this thesis—the by-now familiar ones of his earlier clinical experiences and those deriving from the turbulent period of the late 1960s, which he encountered at first hand, both in the United States and in Germany, in his personal as well as in his professional life.

Chapter 11

Mental Health Aspects of Rapid Social Change

In the winter of 1959-1960, Lindemann was assigned by the Mental Health Section of the World Health Organization to India to study and make recommendations regarding the teaching of psychiatry in Indian medical schools. He felt very deeply the need to strive personally for world peace and universal brotherhood and saw participation in a United Nations program as instrumental to this end. India also presented an opportunity to evaluate his mental health concepts in terms of a non-Western culture.

Having wrestled with his own culture shock in India, he was able to view from another vantage point the complacency with which Americans have wished to export their "efficient industrial democratic pattern," to see this pattern as linked to a particular stage in technological development, and to respect the preference of Eastern societies for their own methods of child-rearing and psychotherapy. At the same time he perceived an important role for the culturally sophisticated psychiatrist, psychologist or, public health worker who would recognize the opportunities for preventive intervention inherent in the massive social changes taking place in the developing countries.

His awakened interest in these issues led to his subsequent participation in two Asia-oriented conferences: a meeting of the Urbanization Advisory Committee of the South Pacific Commission in 1961 and the Conference on Mental Health Research in Asia and the Pacific at Honolulu in 1966. Chapter 11 is based on the paper he gave at the latter conference, where the presence of investigators from developed and developing countries sharpened some of the differences in approach.

The discussion of mental health issues both in practice and research would be incomplete without a consideration of the social matrix in which disordered behavior occurs. In counting the number of psychiatric conditions in any given population, one is inclined to think of the social structure as relatively static with little change over time. Over the last two decades, however, we have learned to view social systems, whether at the community, family, or group level, as dynamic organizations subject to continual change, faster in some segments of the structure and slower in others. Casualties are expected only when rapid changes occur in individual opportunities and role expectations and in collective arrangements for the maintenance of the social order.

The scope of mental health considerations must be broadened to include casualties involving not only the psychoses, psychoneuroses, and psychosomatic disorders but also persons who fail to function effectively as useful members of society. It is this range of casualty that must be considered in planning for urban change, patterns of industrialization, and manpower procurement and providing facilities for newcomers at the time of rapid population shifts.

The sociology of knowledge has taught us to distinguish

different types of professional organization. Among psychiatrists there are at least two forms of interest and professional behavior. One group, working in mental hospitals where persons with disturbed behavior have been segregated for the protection of others and to some degree of themselves, has been concerned with methods of case finding, prediction of case loads in order to make adequate provision of hospital facilities, and determination of the rates of return of persons able to reenter the community. These psychiatrists are interested particularly in severe cases requiring maximum effort for their care and treatment.

The interests characterizing the psychiatrists of the second group started from the study of the psychogenic forms of somatic disorders. Their initial interest was in hypnosis and psychotherapy, but it was later extended to a dynamic interpretation of the social and motivational factors leading to disordered behavior. Recently, their concern with the social factors influencing motivation and disturbed emotional equilibrium has developed into a study of events of social change. These interests also have led to the study of the effect of early psychological experience on personality growth and development in primates in addition to humans in the hope of finding clues to preventive measures in infant care, family organization, and social planning.

The conference from which this paper evolved constituted in itself an event that could accelerate social change by altering the mental health arrangements in Eastern or Western countries as a consequence of sharing the findings and methods in this wide field. Although social change in the Western industrialized countries has been equated automatically with improvement and success, many Eastern countries are concerned with controls against too rapid and ill-advised arrangements for change that would destroy significant values of the past and undermine existing communal safeguards for emotional well-being and assistance in times of life crises. The recurrent theme of dependency in interpersonal relations and the value of a supportive network in kinship and community in Eastern approaches, in contrast to the Western idea of the independent, autonomous individual who can adapt to a great variety of circumstances, serves as a warning not to oversimplify notions about social change, as though psychiatry and mental health in the East were expected to take over without drastic revision the conceptual orientation and the methods of behavioral scientists of the West. Among Easterners there seems to be a wish to underline the existence of value patterns with respect to social relations and individual support, a point that should be carefully considered by Westerners.

I propose to review briefly some of the essentials of the organization of caretaking and maintenance functions in social systems that provide for the survival of the community and the majority of its members, even if at the cost of different access to opportunities and differential exposure to social stress. Then I will consider certain forms of drastic social change which, no matter where they occur, challenge the adaptive potential of group members. Such change may lead to casualties as well as to forms of social learning, as can be well demonstrated in the study of bereavement reactions. It can be illustrated by two forms of planned social change as seen in arrangements for the reception of newcomers in a middle-class suburb in contrast to the arrangements for the displacement of a slum population at the time of urban renewal. In both instances, it appears that the fate of the individuals and the likelihood of their developing unfortunate behavior reactions, including mental disease, depends on the way in which the various professions in the community collaborate; health services often become involved only after many other things have gone wrong and the individual's breakdown is in a late stage.

It may be of interest to consider for a moment how the

medical profession relates to other caretaking professions in a society. Medical and health services and professional activities can be regarded as constituting certain prerogatives of access to a segment of the population that becomes eligible for such services by exhibiting a certain kind of behavior. Parsons (1958) has described such behavior in some detail as the "sick role." Much effort has been spent on circumscribing behavior to fit into disease categories, thereby establishing without question the right, as well as the obligation, of the health services to segregate this population as "their" cases. However, the boundary between these services and other community agencies and professions is fluid, and it determines much of the uncertainty about the nature and care of disturbing, undesirable, and suffering individuals, particularly at times of rapid social change. These relationships are diagramed here.

The medical profession likes to be the gatekeeper to all those who can be defined as sick. They vie in this prerogative with at least four other professional or quasi-professional groups in the community, each of which has an important separate function. In Western countries there is, at the present time, much discussion about whether alcoholism and drug addiction constitute diseases to be handled by medical methods or forms of criminal behavior to be handled by punishment and deterrent methods. Many forms of intense preoccupation with fantasy life in Eastern countries can be considered withdrawal into a religious world of traditional imagery, but these may also constitute an illness incapacitating the person for effective collaboration in the social order. Priests and shamans both have long traditions about permissible and objectionable forms of withdrawal from social participation, and their methods of treatment or restoration to acceptable conduct vie with approaches of scientific medicine. In different societies, an equilibrium develops between different professional groups that is liable to displacement in the process of social change (Lebra 1969, Sasaki 1969).

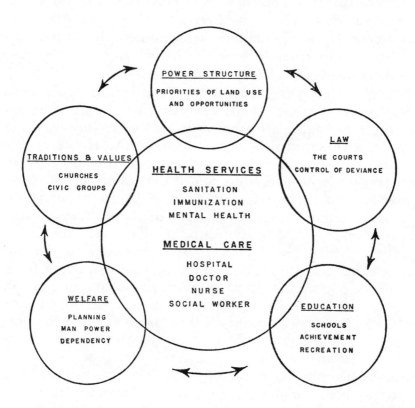

Figure 1

Furthermore, there are the ubiquitious societal arrangements for child-rearing and education of new members of
society and for assistance to members who are unsuccessful in
self-support or in helping their families. These areas of education and welfare again have their own definition of permissible

and nonpermissible deviance. The underachiever in school may be considered lazy and in need of punishment or sick and in need of medical care. The chronically unemployed person may be considered a legitimate beggar, a punishable pauper, or a person to be counseled and in whose favor opportunities should be rearranged. Again, the point at which a pattern of conduct becomes a legitimate concern of the medical profession is uncertain, and it shifts from society to society. Furthermore, a style of dealing with emotions, particularly aggression, is developed and enforced through tradition and child-rearing methods, as have been described in the case of Burma (Spiro 1969, Weidman 1969) and Pakistan (Zaidi 1969).

One of the most significant developments in mental health research both in the West and in the East seems to be the gradual acceptance of social science concepts and procedures for the description and interpretation across cultures of potentially comparable patterns of child-rearing, educational arrangements for individual welfare, control of deviance, and distribution of opportunities for growth and satisfaction. It is now possible to forget about rivalries and mutual derogation between different professional groups and to recognize the common concerns and the many occasions for cooperation in the recognition and care of emotional disturbances.

Events of drastic social change have been of particular interest precisely because the relative contributions to effective problem solving by various professional groups could be appraised and bridges for understanding could be found. Social changes caused by bereavement—that is, the loss of an emotionally significant member of an intimate social network—have been the object of a number of studies (Chapter 4, Engel 1960, Schmale 1958). It has been possible to circumscribe the processes of mourning and grief and to delineate the adaptive and maladaptive consequences both for the individuals and for social groups. Diagnosis under such circumstances refers not so much to a disease picture as to categories of disturbed behavior relating to the time and sequence of psychological events expected after such crises. A variety of disease pictures—psychosomatic, psychoneurotic, criminal behavior, and identifiable psychosis—can then be referred to as adaptive patterns in the mastery of a particular crisis of rapid social change. It was Adolf Meyer who pointed out that it is indispensable in assessment and diagnosis of any sort of disordered behavior to study the adaptive crisis at hand, the equipment and resources of the individual and his group to deal with it, and the role of the psychiatrist as a participating caretaker, who has to mesh his efforts with those of other professional and nonprofessional persons with other responsibilities for the disturbed person's life. A comprehensive diagnosis obviously demands much more investment of time and effort than is possible in the frame of population surveys.

John Gordon at the Harvard School of Public Health used to point out that contemporary psychiatry counts behavior patterns in much the same way that decades ago forms of hives might have been counted as symptoms of infectious disease. A bold statement could be made that patterns of disordered behavior involve not individuals but clusters of individuals related to one another in meaningful ways; that much of the disturbance results from feelings, expectations, and responses of others to the individual under consideration; and that for mental health work the development of sociopathology is a necessary correlate to that of individual pathology. Studies of particular constellations possibly preceding the development of psychosomatic disease, such as ulcerative colits following bereavement, led to the recognition of pathogenic social settings. In cases of ulcerative colitis, excessive dependence on a special type of mother may be found; or in schizophrenia, defective patterns of communication may exist in the family structure.

The intervention of the psychiatrist becomes, then, an effort at dealing with forms of social pathology that are precursors to more severe forms of disturbed behavior. Efforts to categorize the pathology of social systems, including families, and the periods of disorganization that can be expected at times of rapid change are just beginning.

It is useful to look carefully at the provisions made by communities to deal with the necessary events of social change. I will not review here the large number of studies concerning the rate of mental disorder after migration and change of habitat; excellent overviews have been provided by Murphy (1961) and Fried (1964). Murphy showed dramatically the great diversity of findings that at present are not susceptible to systematic interpretation because of the diversity of methods of counting of casualties and the lack of adequate description of the social processes involved.

Studies on bereavement and separation reactions, as well as the analysis of acculturation problems under a variety of conditions, have shed some light on the complexities of the coping mechanisms involved in role transition and crisis behavior. The work of Engel (1960), Schmale (1958), and Coelho, Hamburg, and Murphy (1963), dealing primarily with individuals and small groups in crisis, encouraged further work concerned with the responses of large population groups. My own concern has been with the details of community arrangements to assist persons in transition (chapter 8), rather than with counting the cases of illness among migrant and nonmigrant members of the population.

In dealing with crises of transition, the psychiatrist, cooperating with other professions, will be called on much less to diagnose mental disorders than to give advice about the best preparation and supportive measures for the most vulnerable segment of the population in crisis. Together with social scientists, he will try to assess the mental health consequences of social processes, such as changes in roles and hierarchy, opportunities for communication, and shifts in prevailing values. The rapid processes of urbanization and industrialization throughout the developing countries in Asia require from the mental health worker a fresh appraisal not only of individual defenses against breakdown but also of the collective attitudes and traditional procedures, such as ceremonials, to be safeguarded.

Several papers presented at the Conference on Mental Health Research in Asia and the Pacific in Honolulu in 1966 showed the serious preoccupation of investigators with cultural phenomena that protect the population to some degree against emotional breakdown but represent at the same time a form of social pathology victimizing certain members of the community; this is well exemplified by the studies of witchcraft (Spiro 1969). There should be careful evaluation of the levels of tolerance for various ways in which certain individuals are made scapegoats in order to satisfy collective paranoid tendencies.

There is also the problem of tolerance for deviant or abnormal behavior. The apparent increase in the number of persons with mental abnormalities of old age, who constitute a very large percentage of those admitted to mental hospitals in the West, appears, according to Gruenberg (1954), to be related to the decreased tolerance of the industrialized society for the presence of the elderly, even when they are only mildly disturbed.

It is clear from all I have been saying that I advocate a change in role and value orientation for the psychiatrist who engages in mental health work. He must still be a fully established clinical diagnostician, but he must also have knowledge of the possible precursors of disease (as exemplified by grief reactions). Together with social scientists, he will have to address himself to social systems, whether family, kinship circle, small group, work-team, institution, or whole community. Problems of transition and crises of adaptation are challenges for the right kind of mental health services, and they are also opportunities for investigation. Bulatao's study (1969) of the multiple facets of gradual acculturation and Westernization in the Philippines illustrates the value of this kind of inquiry.

My experience in a large metropolitan hospital in Boston has shown that such a role change by the psychiatrist is important even for consultation with the other medical departments. Here again, the social processes involved in the arrival and departure of the patient, the social structure of individual wards, and the opportunities for social reintegration of the patient on return to the community have become significant factors in appraising the nature and probable outcome of a given medical condition.

Although each contributor to this conference has presented with pride the accomplishments in his particular sphere of operations, he also has had to come to terms with very great differences in research technology and organization skills. The more advanced is the level of technology, the better the opportunities appear for comparative studies. Epidemiological surveys with respect to clear-cut clinical entities are obviously the most promising. However, the less quantitative, rather exploratory, studies—which combine social science and psychodynamic and clinical observation—do much to develop a high level of motivation and involvement, creating a community of issues that must precede the evolution of methods of collaboration.

REFERENCES

Bulatao, J. (1969). Westernization and the split-level personality in the Filipino. In *Mental Health Research in Asia and the Pacific,* ed. W. Caudill and T-Y Lin, 296-305. Honolulu: East-West Center Press. pp.

Coelho, G.V., Hamburg, D., and Murphy, E.B. (1963). Coping strategies in a new learning environment: a study of American college freshmen. *Archives of General Psychiatry* 9:433-443.

Engel, G.L. (1960). A unified concept of health and disease. *Perspectives in Biology and Medicine* 3:459-485.

Fried, M. (1964). Effects of social change on mental health. *American Journal of Orthopsychiatry* 34:3-28.

Gruenberg, E. (1954). The epidemiology of mental disease. *Scientific American,* March, pp. 38-42.

Lebra, P. (1969). Shaman and client in Okinasa. In *Mental Health Research in Asia and the Pacific,* ed. W. Caudill and T-Y Lin, pp. 216-222. Honolulu: East-West Center Press.

Murphy, H.B.M. (1961). Social change and mental health. *Milbank Memorial Fund Quarterly,* 39:385-445.

Parsons, T. (1958). Some trends of change in American society: their bearing on medical education. *Journal of the American Medical Association* 167:31-36.

Sasaki, Y. (1969). Psychiatric study of the shaman in Japan. In *Mental Health Research in Asia and the Pacific,* ed. W. Caudill and T-Y Lin, pp. 223-241. Honolulu: East-West Center Press.

Schmale, A.H. (1958). Relationship of separation and depression to disease: a report on a hospitalized medical population. *Psychosomatic Medicine* 20:259-277.

Spiro, M.E. (1969). The psychological function of witchcraft belief: the Burmese case. In *Mental Health Research in Asia and the Pacific,* ed. W. Caudill and T-Y Lin, pp. 245-258. Honolulu: East-West Center Press.

Weidman, H.H. (1969). Cultural values, concept of self and projection: the Burmese case. In *Mental Health Research in Asia and the Pacific,* ed. W. Caudill and T-Y Lin, pp. 259-285. Honolulu: East-West Center Press.

Zaidi, S.M.H. (1969). Sociocultural change and value conflict in developing countries: a case study of Pakistan. In *Mental Health Research in Asia and the Pacific*, ed. W. Caudill and T-Y Lin, pp. 415-430. Honolulu: East-West Center Press.

Chapter 12

Ethical Aspects of Culture Change

To understand the background of this paper, given in German at Lindau in May 1968, it is necessary to know something about Lindemann's activities subsequent to his retirement from the Massachusetts General Hospital in the fall of 1965. He accepted an invitation to join Dr. David Hamburg's Department of Psychiatry at Stanford University as Visiting Professor, an arrangement that freed him of administrative responsibilities and made it possible for him to spend more time in his native Germany. There, he had already become a central figure in the annual Lindau Psychotherapy Week, a unique experiment in imparting mental health skills to general practitioners, youth leaders, and other care-giving personnel.

The 1968 session took place in the atmosphere of tension and intergenerational conflict endemic in the United States and Europe throughout the period of the Vietnam war. By developing the theme of the social therapist, Lindemann to some degree enacts a therapeutic role himself by inviting his audience to examine social change dispassionately in its univer-

sal aspects. At the same time, he draws his illustrations mainly
from the medical, rather than from the political, world, basing
them on his recent experiences at the highly research-oriented
medical school at Stanford.

When we speak of culture change we mean that in all sorts of
groups and organizations alterations occur, sometimes slow
and at other times rapid, having to do with life-style, role
patterns, integration of the individual into the society, his
opportunities for achievement or gain, and survival in the
group. Modern anthropologists not only study distant primitive cultures; they also go into our neighborhoods and observe,
in different social classes, ethnic groups and organizations,
how a particular life-style and the way in which people function with each other provide for the continuity of the social
system, which can tolerate many changes but cannot withstand
others.

Alteration and change have become slogans of our time.
Change itself has become a value of the culture through the
technological developments of the last decades. What is already
there appears obsolete: one wants something new. This acceler-
ation of change—especially the astounding development of
science, the task of which is continually to seek for innovation—has brought with it the feeling that today's order and
way of life are unstable and cannot last.

I am glad that Victor von Weizsaecker's *Der kranke Mensch*
was republished (1951). Sixteen years ago it seemed hard to
understand and full of fantasy. But today we are forced to
recognize that he foresaw much of what we now experience as a
challenge—namely, the obligation of the doctor not only to
treat sick individuals but also to see in what way the patient's
need reflects the need of the community. In his time it was still
very doubtful that community needs were accessible by means
of a medical approach. Today, however, von Weizsaecker's
insight has become a challenge to develop a medical ethics.

I would like to describe how a social conscience has led certain doctors to find and develop a new role in the community. In this specialty, which we call *community psychiatry*, one tries not only to treat patients as individuals but also to somehow draw into the field of treatment the community to which this individual belongs and in which he suffers.

Should one, as a conscientious doctor, do something like this? One will only too easily come into conflict with other professions. It is not only the doctor who has concern for the community in which a patient lives; there are also other callings: The pastors, lawyers, judges, politicians, educators, and social workers can be considered community care-givers, looking after the welfare of others. Some receive pay; some feel themselves morally obligated, believing that their conscience pushes them into this caretaking role vis-à-vis their fellow men. When the doctor steps in here and wants to be more than a do-gooding layman, he must have competence and knowledge—just as when he treats individuals—in order to work successfully against disorganization or disturbance in community groups.

Thus, a new professional branch has developed which we might call *social therapy*. This expression is used by Kilian; Margaret Mead (1956) chooses the term "sociatry" in contrast to "psychiatry."

What happens when we leave the hospital or the consulting room and go into the community? I will report about some experiences with various community groups and try to show how we have encountered ethical problems everywhere in the other caretaking professions and in their institutions and how these problems are frequently connected with culture change, either threatened, actual, or recently experienced.

I formerly described mourning as a reaction to the loss of a significant person. We have gradually learned to see that mourning and similar reactions are also sequels to cultural changes. It is almost always true, even in the case of the loss of an individual, that the one who has died and has become unavailable helped to determine the style of life in the community; and the more he determined it, the more he will be missed. The survivor often has to discover a new style. The transition from an old to a new way of life, however, is also a central problem of culture change. One must try to picture what the separate items of such a change consist of. Each organization intent on self-preservation as a social structure must naturally assign certain roles to its members and must clarify its particular division of labor. One must see to it that all have a clear picture of the role each person plays, that each member has the right to expect something from every one else, and that these expectations are fulfilled to some extent. If they are not fulfilled, disturbances occur. And one always finds more or less visible arrangements to cope with the loss of members and facilitate the taking over of roles by new participants.

Thus, the death of an executive will lead to a disturbance in social equilibrium if one has not planned carefully for such a transition. One will indeed find mourning and feelings of loss on the part of many people—but also anxiety lest the wrong man take his place. One must be sure that only certain persons with the right qualifications but also with the right value orientation come into the organization. It frequently turns out that an outsider seems far less dangerous than many persons who are already in the system, and who may unfortunately be known only too well!

Similarly in family life, the death of father or mother can have many meanings for young children. Perhaps he or she disappeared deliberately, out of ill will; perhaps he can come back, and one must keep a place in the family free for him (Clark 1966). And one also discovers that the particular way in which a father or a mother determined the family's style just cannot be replaced. The problem then becomes one of finding a new style, perhaps through a parent surrogate or possibly with a completely different role distribution in the life of the group. Bowlby has made careful observations of what happens to children when an important person, particularly the mother, disappears from the family constellation.

In such cases the doctor's role is fairly clear. When he deals with parents whose child has an incurable illness or with a child whose father has just died, he knows approximately what a socially oriented therapist should do. One can provide opportunity for grieving and thus prevent maladaptive developments. We also know something about how the process of making substitutions in personal relationships can be regulated. However, in our collaboration with colleagues in other departments, we find that this kind of intervention in crises of the social structure seems new and strange to them. When we come as a social psychiatrist to our hospital colleagues on a ward where a patient is going to die, we frequently find an unpleasant tension, as if they had a troubled conscience. "Should we perhaps send for a pastor? But which one? Perhaps the patient is a Catholic; but at the moment we don't have a Catholic priest. Could we help out a Catholic with a non-Catholic clergyman? No, that doesn't work. Should the doctor speak to him? Wait a minute, there's the psychiatrist! He must know what to do—he knows something about grief work!"

And indeed, the psychiatrist in his new role is interested. He knows that terminal care brings with it ethically and morally complicated situations. One not only faces the reality that medical help has failed, but one must also raise the question, When does one mention it and to whom? Should one possibly tell the relatives and not the patient? The social scientists declare, however, that open communication is extremely important in a critical situation. If one only tells the family and not the patient, a channel of communication between them is prematurely interrupted. For if they cannot speak about death, the most important subject at the moment, they will not talk about anything else meaningful either.

So we are involved in the area of human relationships with counsel as well as with moral questions, for we are advocates for the well-being of all concerned. That often means the nurses, who may find themselves in the intensive-care unit in a situation where they are intermediaries between the doctor, the patient, and the family. They too may think that they should not say anything about death, even though the doctor gives official permission. The whole system of roles in which they are carefully schooled—the status relationship between doctor and nurse—is then disturbed, and they are afraid to do something the doctor really should do himself.

If we encourage nurses to take over elements of the doctor's role, in terms of such ethical questions, it is with the awareness that on the larger scene the professional role of the nurse is taking on a new significance, that her area of competence is enlarged, and that her profession, like so many other helping professions, is currently undergoing culture change, at least in America and probably in Europe as well. The nurse—who hitherto was involved in bedside care, looking after the physical and psychological needs of the patient—now increasingly is assuming a technical function. She controls pieces of apparatus, she interprets complicated data, and she services highly developed instruments. She becomes a first-class technician and, so to speak, a scientist. And as a scientist, she stands over against the doctor, who also derives his pride from applied science, as an almost equal member of the medical team.

When the nurse comes nearer to the doctor in this role shift, the problem of professional distance arises. On a psychiatric ward, where one used to consider her a dependent employee, the nurse may become the central figure in the social system, from whose decisions the welfare of the patient will be directly influenced. Formerly, she only gave reports; now she takes a conscious part in decision making.

With the culture change in the psychiatric hospital, such as comes about through the development of the *therapeutic milieu,* a significant role shift takes place and is experienced as an ethical or moral problem; many doctors can cope with it, whereas others cannot. A series of disturbances, ethical issues, and conflicts that developed when such a milieu was created in Cambridge, England, has recently been described by Clark (1966). It turned out that all concerned—not only the patients but also the nurses, assistants, and doctors, especially the residents—went through a period of disturbance that they experienced as uncertainty over what was required and what was permitted. Seeing such disturbances as the result not of personal failure but of a change in the social system seems to us the key to a new ethics.

In an historical period when participation is demanded from groups that formerly had no voice and formerly had as their main role to carry out directions in a conscientious manner—a period in which collaboration and joint decision making are expected from patients and clients—many situations can be observed as presenting the symptoms of a far-reaching culture change. Such situations are almost always accompanied by feelings of discomfort, anxiety, and even guilt. If one can then put the blame on somebody, one immediately feels much better!

And so it is frequently one of our tasks to emphasize that blaming particular individuals in situations of rapid culture change as the originators of anxiety reactions and tensions is usually unfair. The problem for us as social therapists then consists of studying those transition periods as one studies a case history. Then we see crises, not of an individual life, but of the social order, with its value orientations, role distribution, and hierarchical positions. We can identify the beginnings, the precipitating situation, the first symptoms, the systemic disturbance, the culmination, and finally the reordering of the common enterprise. If reorganization does not succeed, the system falls apart or is replaced by other institutions. When we learn to bring this kind of social pathology into connection with the pathology of the individual, we will be able to understand many stubborn forms of illness that currently resist treatment.

The social therapist finds another form of culture change as a sequel to the rapid technological development of medicine. The hospital and especially the teaching hospital, which until recently existed for the care and treatment of sufferers, now appear to the patients more and more as a conglomeration of laboratories, in which scientists hope to make important discoveries, using the patients as welcome subjects of their experiments. When many patients show reluctance and a social psychiatrist is called in, the latter finds that an important change in the role of the sick person has taken place. Many of these patients did not come because they needed help at this particular time but were invited because they had an interesting illness. They have an arrangement with the doctor or hospital director to stay there and be thoroughly examined for scientific purposes. However, this completely alters their position. They no longer have the attitudes and expectations of the obedient patient. They know that the doctor is experimenting on them in some way; their suffering may benefit future generations, but not them and their family in the immediate present. The nurses, social workers, and physicians know this too; but we act as if the patient still has the obligation to fit into the treatment plan obediently and thankfully.

When one comes as a social therapist into a research-oriented ward, one senses immediately that the new social climate has produced uncertainty and confusion in all concerned and that the rules for intake, treatment, and discharge are different. For example, the patient will not be discharged because he is better but because the experiment is finished. All must learn new roles and alter their demands and expectations if they wish to prevent recurring unrest and disturbances.

The doctors are convinced that they are doing their best in the cause of science. They are working for the future, and can be proud of their achievements, such as heart and kidney transplantations. However, it turns out that such new procedures are so complicated from an ethical and moral point of view, with respect to the well-being of the patient and his relatives, that the surgeons have become quite concerned about them. The social therapist then discovers that medical science also is fitted into a system of cultural values that are in the throes of rapid change. For example, there is the problem of publishing scientific achievements in the newspapers or over television and radio. The issue of competition arises: Who did it first? And the question no longer is whether the problem of immunity reactions after a heart transplant has been solved. When a surgeon in South Africa publishes his achievements, the doctors in the United States are quite unhappy because they are still deeply engaged in the preparatory phases. Many hospitals will then suddenly undertake heart transplantations that will be considered premature by certain specialists.

Somehow what I call the "industrialization of science" has entered into this competition among scientists. The profit in this case is prestige. And in our time, prestige is an important goal one must often purchase at the cost of ethical values.

If we social psychiatrists have the opportunity to be present as participant observers when a critical procedure such as a kidney or heart transplantation is taking place, we try to clarify the interpersonal and ethical problems of all those concerned. One may find that the psychological aspects appear quite complicated on the part of the organ donor and his family. With heart transplantation, the donor, of course, is dead, and it is a question of finding new criteria for the precise moment of death, which all must subscribe to. But even when the donor is living, ethical and psychological questions arise. We have studied carefully the motivation of people who want to donate their kidneys. These were not at all a random group of people but often were hysterical girls who had a special psychological capacity to dispose of their bodies. They were girls at a period of their lives in which a bodily restitution for a real or imagined guilt seemed required, and so they gave their kidneys to pacify their conscience. It was thus extremely important to them that the recipient of their organ survived. If he should die, it would all have been in vain, and they would have failed again.

There did indeed turn out to be serious ethical problems with respect to donors. One found an alteration of their family structure, as they had developed a remarkable sense of relationship to the recipient. Because one shared a kidney, an identification took place. The problem of a shared identity with the heart transplant patients is also interesting. The bodily relatedness to a stranger who uses the heart of a deceased family member for his own survival complicates the grief process of the family members.

These examples suffice to indicate the new area in which socially oriented therapists are working. In all these situations, the consultant tries to grasp the precise nature of the social structure and social processes. He focuses on the role distribution, patterns of communication, and status hierarchy. At the same time, he must continually assess the value orientations and ethical expectations of all the participants in the social system. It is often possible, through such a situational analysis, to recognize that guilt feelings, fear, and scapegoating of others are situationally determined and inappropriate and may be replaced by renewed efforts at adaptation and social reorganization. Just as in individual therapy when defense mechanisms with their varied forms of guilt and anxiety become manifest as formerly justified but now unsuitable, so in social therapy a careful analysis of the distinctions between former and current social situations reveals anxiety, bitterness, and inappropriate guilt feelings, which are determined by the culture change, and leads to attempts to master the new situation through common efforts.

The rapid culture change in the medical world, which we have discussed here, is only a small element of the great wave of social change affecting other important institutions and professions. In schools and universities and in the churches and welfare bureaus, new expectations are everywhere occurring, along with a new serious consideration of the complementary roles allocated to people through privilege and disadvantage, through wealth and poverty, through distinctions of race and age. The professions of applied sociology and anthropology, like the social therapist in the medical sphere, try to come to grips, through situational analysis, with the expectations and protest activities of the young people and the more or less violent attempts of minorities to force social change. In these research efforts, too, the collaboration of the clinically trained psychotherapist turns out to be useful. For example, a psychiatrist, Dr. John Spiegel (1967), at Brandeis University has worked out a careful situational analysis of the riots in the Negro quarters of certain American cities, in which the origin of hate and accusation was shown to be related to specific phases of the culture change of recent years. With new theoretical understanding of these events, we can modestly hope for new forms of peaceful accommodation at times of social change.

REFERENCES

Clark, D.H. (1966). *Administrative Therapy*. Philadelphia: J.B. Lippincott.
Mead, M. (1956). *New Lives for Old*. New York: Morrow.
Spiegel, J.P. (1967). Race relations and violence: a social psychiatric perspective. *Social Psychiatry: Proceedings of the*

Association for Nervous and Mental Diseases. Baltimore:
Williams and Wilkins.
Von Weizsaecker, V. (1951). *Der kranke Mensch.* Stuttgart: K.F.
Koehler Verlag.

Chapter 13

A Clinical Approach to Institutional Change

Unlike the speech in the chapter 12, which was given on a formal occasion, the two talks that have been combined in this chapter took place in staff meetings with mental health colleagues and were intended to share Lindemann's now-matured conclusions about the psychiatrist's role in a time of social turmoil. The consultation experiences from which he was able to distil the point of view expressed here were many and varied. His assignment by the World Health Organization to consult regarding the teaching of psychiatry in Indian medical schools and his participation in conferences on urbanization in Asia and the Pacific have already been mentioned. In Germany he was widely sought after as a consultant. A three-month appointment at the University of Tuebingen in 1966 gave him insight into the forces associated with change in the German academic community, and he later served consultation engagements at the University of Freiburg and repeatedly at Heidelberg, his Alma Mater.

At Stanford he was at some risk of being co-opted by the more aggressively change-oriented elements of the medical school students and faculty. To maintain a constructively neutral stance required great self-discipline. This was even more the case at Boston College, where he was Visting Professor of Community Psychiatry during the period when the Community-University Center for Inner City Change was being pioneered by the Psychology Department, under the leadership of a former colleague, Dr. J. M. Von Felsinger. In all this he was sustained, as the following remarks show, by his faith in the methods he had used with clinical patients.

A psychiatrist is one who, by training and experience, in an encounter with one or more other persons can encourage them to be their best selves—to be able to deal with their emotional impediments, with that network of conflicting obligations and decisions that have preceded the present situation, and with the alternatives that are open or closed for the future. He is concerned with the direction in which our culture of technology and democracy is moving, seemingly toward setting a high priority on behavior control in the interests of those in power; and he would like to protect the opportunities for being a psychiatrist in this sense of being an enabling person vis-à-vis other individuals.

He also has political objectives: he wishes to make *concern for people* a first priority of social planning. His interest in collectivities is not primary but derives from his concern for human beings embedded in a social system that places them under pressure. He may be perceived, and may actually become, a spokesman for people in trouble to the extent that he is trying to arrange a moratorium, some room in which to maneuver, by termporarily removing the most intense pressures which have got them into crisis—for example, pressures from the authorities, from a tight schedule, or from having to make an immediate all-or-none decision. Hence, he risks being identified by the Establishment with the cause of the underdog. And he himself may be tempted to assume the role of advocate for persons or groups who are trying, legitimately or illegitimately, to manipulate the Establishment.

This temptation may be seen as similar to one experienced during a phase of clinical training, when young therapists go through periods of overidentification with a patient or client, rather than helping him to be more effective in using his own resources. Traditionally, the psychiatrist is required, at such a juncture, to reaffirm his professional role by preserving social anonymity or by reasserting his own position in the social order, reminding himself that he is an agent of that order even though he may sympathize with the person who wishes it to be different. We cannot, in our professional roles, become the promoters or enforcers of social action because, if we do, we are operating in an area in which we do not have the competence on which to rely in making decisions. We are not trained as agitators or union organizers or even (with the exception of some social workers) as community development experts.

However, in our eagerness to foster progress toward a fairer, more compassionate society, we may easily overlook the fact that the changes constantly taking place all around us in communities and institutions are accompanied by many opportunities for the use of our clinical skills. And a number of roles are available that are compatible with our ethical motivation, our professional training, and, it is hoped, with our self-preservation in the system!

The psychiatrist who assumes one of these roles needs specialized knowledge, whether he thinks of himself as a social therapist, an ombudsman or mediator, a mental health consultant, or even an "absurd healer," to borrow Dumont's expression (1968). He will encounter typical situations in which a group tries to achieve a social goal but in the course of it becomes busy stereotyping individuals, name-throwing, fighting not only outsiders but each other, and finally breaking down all channels of communication. Having acquired the ability to deal in therapy with acting-out patients, accepting their anxiety and aggression without counterreacting, he will easily recognize the phenomenon of collective transference and will also see that there are collective, constructive coping arrangements. Although he will not function as a group therapist in such situations, he will have an expert understanding of group processes. Above all, he will understand the conditions under which trust is developed and maintained (Ilfield and Lindemann 1971).

The mediator role belongs not only to psychiatry, but also to experts who are able to develop the required constellation of skills, based on psychiatric theory and practice as well as on the other social sciences. It requires some understanding of the theory of culture change as it affects populations exposed to new settings. When a group with a peasant culture, for example, is displaced into an urban setting, it must accommodate collectively to the core culture while at the same time defending its traditional life style and values (Gans 1962). If such a group is relocated and scattered into small subunits throughout the metropolitan perimeter, one finds these people sick, not in the original psychiatric sense, but as victims of a cultural disaster. One sees them in the throes of recapturing some fragments of a culture, trying to rebuild and make a cohesion out of them (see chapter 11).

Whether one considers the fate of American Indians, deprived of their lands and traditional culture, of Black Southerners driven by changes in agricultural technology into the cities, or of patients who may be the victims of competition among scientists (chapter 12), one wishes to become a spokesman against social evil and for these people. How, then, does one redefine one's role—not in the sense of social action, but in the sense of anticipating the untoward psychological consequences, the by-products of certain ways of behaving, by which the free enterprise society brings about these disasters?

One is fortunate if, as has been my case since I retired from Harvard, one is permitted to be a participant observer in situations where there is pleading for social change and some degree of compliance on the part of the authorities to accommodate it. I think of the ombudsman as a mediator between a power structure and those within it who arrive at the lower rungs and would like to have their grievances heard and acted upon. When Stanford University established the ombudsman position, Katchadourian (1971), a psychiatrist, was able in this role to have access to information on both sides of an encounter and to counsel both sides to be their "best selves," rather than persisting in a power struggle in which the weaker side will obviously lose, short of bringing about chaos and destruction. Helping the individuals engaged in a problem of social betterment to deal with their emotional tensions and to keep the channels of communication open means helping them to be more effective.

With increasing experience in situational analysis, one learns to anticipate some common denominators in the institutional response to change. Take, for example, instances of *innovation*. How does a staff react when it must modernize to secure the acclaim of the reference group? What model is the trainee to choose, in order to be recognized and appreciated?

In response to the crisis of changing institutional values, various defensive reactions occur, including patterns of withdrawal, attack, and submission. There may be overt protest, with or without resultant exit from the system. There may be varying degrees of identification with the change agents and their values. One person may withdraw and even go to sleep in lectures or departmental meetings. Another may adopt the "new look" and cooperate as conspicuously as possible. Yet another could simply change his terminology without altering basic principles of practice—such as speaking of "coping mechanisms" instead of "defenses."

If the innovation occurs in the context of an effort to accommodate a minority group by making institutional changes, one must be prepared for a number of different phases, in some of which "confrontation" will occur. For example, a college decides to establish an outpost in the inner city, where graduate students will collaborate with ghetto residents to help them improve their political and economic position. At the same time, a number of young people from the ghetto, who do not possess the usual academic qualifications, will be admitted to the college's graduate program. The project is inaugurated with generous funding, good publicity, and high expectations. What happens?

In one such program, white graduate students who attempted to make common cause with Black activists were asked to demonstrate that they were not "racists" by performing a number of trivial, if not actually demeaning, tasks. Their natural reaction was one of role confusion and resentment, until they realized that this test of token "slavery" was not a personal insult but a kind of collective compensation that appeared valid in an historical context. Another confrontation took place when the Black graduate students were enrolled in T-groups with white students. So much aggression was mobilized that it was impossible for the whites to continue in the group. (In retrospect, it seems as if a task-oriented type of discussion might have been productive, rather than permitting group members to talk about each other.)

In the face of so much aggression, the project's social system fragmented and became paranoid. Distrust and competitiveness took the place of collaboration with peers and faculty. Ideological schisms deepened. Students decided that they could perform leadership roles better than the faculty. Dissatisfaction began to center on the project's director. He, in turn, instead of seeing this development as a usual aspect of the process of change, felt betrayed and hurt. He reacted with anger and joined in a dispute over tenure rights, which further fragmented the system. Ultimately, he had to leave, as have several other directors of similar enterprises. Here, then, seems to be a common denominator of institutional change: the tendency in a time of innovation to see the original innovator as a progress-impeder who must be got rid of.

With foreknowledge of the organizational stresses that are a usual part of innovation and the change process and of the tendency to consolidate staff frustrations and personify them in the person of the leader, perhaps a way could be found of ritually, rather than actually, sacrificing him. We should anticipate the possible need for shifting leadership at some point in project development and build flexibility into the system, so that there could be alternatives other than losing the leader or the project. If reorganization is necessary for coping and growth, there should be some arrangement for allowing the initiator of change to vacate the directorship with ceremonial grace and with the option of returning at a different level in a different role.

To hold an organization together, there must be overriding social concern and common purpose. Without dedication and shared task orientation, structural, as well as functional, changes can occur in the system. In a general hospital, for example, with the shift to an emphasis on scientific discoveries, the organization can regress from a generally collaborative culture to a mosaic of competitive enterprises, with each group striving for its own status and funds.

All those involved in an institutional identity crisis should consider the situation in historical perspective, and adopt the general position of waiting it out. It is a mistake to think that any particular crisis is the one to end all crises! In every instance, the future of the institution's value setters is uncertain, too. There tends to be pendular shifting in the prestige of particular goals and principles of practice. The pendulum swings, and in time the scene changes. Regardless of the vicissitudes of status and prestige, psychodynamics continue to be operative, and good clinical practitioners are always needed.

An institution committed to change or constituted to pursue innovative goals is wise to anticipate the probable need for an administratively oriented mental health consultant. Although employed by the power structure, it is important that he not have executive functions. He should be a fringe person who is trustworthy and can function as a participant observer. Like a good therapist, he can point out things that otherwise go unnoticed, such as long-range versus short-range interests. An administrative consultant must operate at all levels in an organization if he is to be maximally useful. His main task is to keep channels of communication open. He must be able to make another segment of the organization aware of stresses without carrying tales.

There are ethical problems for the consultant, because he is employed by the institution to facilitate change but to keep the forces of change in some bounds. After all, the Establishment must find meaningful accommodation between the protagonists of various current issues: clinical versus research, Black versus white, professional versus paraprofessional, and men versus women.

Often, organizations that are involved in rapid social change only appreciate the need for administrative mental health consultation when their system is already sick, and it may then be too late. If the consultant has been included from the beginning, he has developed trustful relationships at various levels. This may not be possible if already there is severe fragmentation and polarization. When trust lapses, the consultant as well as others may be sacrificed.

To sum up, one would hope that knowledge of the process of

social change might help organizations to "roll with the punches," as a therapist does with an excessively anxious and demanding patient. By anticipating the particular difficulties and needs of periods of innovation, many individual casualties can be prevented, and whole projects saved from becoming failures.

On another level, a preventive psychiatrist would search out the original contributing factors that result in a rising casualty rate in some segment of the population and become concerned, like Leonard Duhl (1963), with planning and innovation as a participant in the decision-making process. For example, one would anticipate the consequences of mass migrations to the cities and try to deal with the life needs of the people so that they would not become uprooted. Could communities be built that would give different elements of our population the opportunity to preserve their cultural values and their life-styles, rather than having a uniform life-style dictated by the power-elite? I am thinking of intentional communities, such as the Amana people, the Fabian cultures, or the Bruderhof. We experiment with growing bacilli on an agar medium, Could we attempt experiments in human culture?

In the preventive role, one must be able to communicate not only with the disenfranchised people but also with those planners and business people who possess the resources of the society, to persuade them to use these in health-fostering ways. How can the people who are despondent get enough of a voice vis-à-vis the power-elite so that they can be heard and not be perceived as destructive or revolutionary? As the value system of our contemporary society is based on competitive individual aggrandizement, we are likely to feed back most of our resources into greater aggrandizement of the entrepreneur, rather than into schemes to help people. We need modulators, a knowledgeable segment of the Establishment, who are concerned about the human and cultural catastrophes that are by-products of the system and that could be studied and controlled just as we try to control the side effects of drugs in medicine.

It is obvious that much research is needed to buttress social planning, but the new information has to be used with due regard for the existing power structure and for the equilibrium of ongoing social processes. The determinants of priorities for planning and action are as unconscious, as powerful, as complex, and as difficult to reach as are the unconscious forces in the individual psychic apparatus. Their clarification depends on the joint efforts of psychiatrists and social scientists acting in close collaboration.

As in psychotherapy, the task of intervening in social forces is a matter of dealing with resistances; an existing balance may be upset, and the social therapist may have the vexing problem of deciding not only what information is relevant but also when it is useful and when it is destructive. There is much evidence that the untimely use of information can result in hostility, destructive responses, and retardation of progress (Lindemann 1965). We must not be surprised that social science investigation is often taken as spying, that persons in power will label certain data as classified, or that persons being questioned are reluctant to divulge more or less private information for fear it might be used against them.

The vaunted claim of scientific endeavor to be objective and free from value bias is seriously challenged whenever social information goes beyond the clarification of principles for general policy and preempts decision making. The social scientist—and even more so, the psychiatrist—who becomes a consultant to leaders of political or social action can be easily tempted to succumb to twin dangers: the preferential use of information and the disregard of other data to suit the value priorities of the ruling groups.

A new area of serious and difficult work lies before us. There will certainly be many disappointments, and our present optimism may turn out not to be justified. I believe, however, that in the ward as well as the office and in the open community as well as in institutions, the psychotherapeutic attitude and psychodynamic insight that make it possible for the doctor to be tolerant, to listen, to postpone decisions, and to permit clients and patients to participate responsibly in new solutions and new social arrangements are basic prerequisites for work in the social field.

REFERENCES

Duhl, L. (1963). Introduction. In *The Urban Condition*, ed. L.J. Duhl, pp. vii-xiii. New York: Basic Books.

Dumont, M. (1968). *The Absurd Healer: Perspectives of a Community Psychiatrist.* New York: Jason Aronson.

Gans, H.J. (1962). *The Urban Villagers.* New York: Free Press of Glencoe.

Ilfeld, F.W., and Lindemann, Erich (1971). Professional and community: pathways toward trust. *American Journal of Psychiatry* 128:583-589.

Katchadourian, H.A. (1971). The psychiatrist as university ombudsman. Stanford University.

Lindemann, Erich (1965). Social system factors as determinants of resistance to change. *American Journal of Psychiatry* 35:544-556.

Part V

Epitome

Introduction to Part V

by Dr. David Satin

At this stage, Erich Lindemann's life and work had come full circle. In the first phase he had integrated intimations of his own life losses and adaptations with his studies of neurophysiological reactions. Then followed the objective observation of patterns of coping with life crises and the accompanying insistence that concern for environmental stresses and resources be incorporated into mental health training and practice. In the final period, his understanding of social process had expanded and deepened, along with his perception of the professional's role in and contribution to it. And now the ultimate test: Do the concepts of life crisis, coping capacity, and environmental resources apply to the conceptualizer himself?

In facing the stress of his terminal illness, Erich Lindemann offers himself as a living example of the interrelationship of patient and helping agents in mutual understanding and coping. There is no hierarchy of roles or linear sequence of action, but a dynamic interchange of realities in which patient, therapist, and family *share* (one of his favorite words) the task and the consequences—indeed as a community dealing with mental health issues. The example and his articulation of it are the epitome of his thinking and teaching.

Chapter 14

Reactions to One's Own Fatal Illness

Even if he had said nothing worthwhile, the scene would have been impressive: the professor who was also a patient standing in the narrow, windowless room in the basement of the Stanford Medical School, where he had recently been undergoing radiation therapy, before a small group of residents, technicians, and nurses. He had had a sacral chordoma for six years and would have two more years of unspeakable suffering. He could have been excused for withdrawing, but giving came as naturally to him as breathing.

Those present on that February morning in 1972 heard him thank them for their unsuccessful efforts at curing him. If they had been trying to avoid thinking about what having terminal cancer meant to some of the people they were treating, they now heard of several ways to help these patients come to better terms with prospective death.

David Satin has called this chapter "the ultimate expression of Dr. Lindemann's characteristic openness with others and the clearest statement of his companionship and sharing with the patient as his therapeutic stance."

I am delighted to have the opportunity to express my appreciation for the fact that I am able to be here, without much discomfort, and able to be an active participant in academic life again. I came here last November looking for help; I was quite crippled as far as my activities went because of pain and general discomfort. It would be only natural for me, since I am in that branch of medicine that deals with experiences and subjective states, to talk a bit about how patients feel, in general, when they are confronted with approaching death, mediated through a malignancy or other conditions; and say a little how a particular kind of person, of my age and attitude and values, reacted to the confrontation with the situation. I should like to mention that it was Mrs. Lutzker, the department social worker, who first suggested that I talk about this theme. Her daily presence in the radiation service was one of the very important items of the treatment experience, to which I shall refer later.

How does one get to the problem, confrontation with death? At the Massachusetts General Hospital, where I worked for thirty years, we came to it through our interest in how people react to losing part of their body—partial death. We studied women who had had a hysterectomy. They found themselves reacting with surprising distress to this event: Instead of being grateful to their surgeon, they were furious with him! One of these women was admitted to our Psychiatry Service after having knocked her surgeon flat on the floor on the follow-up visit; she was so scared that her fist would fly out again that she said, "Help me against this violent impulse!" And so we became interested, and our first study was of a series of women who had had hysterectomies, comparing them with patients who had had cholecystectomies. And it turned out that indeed they experienced a heightened level of violence and hostile feelings, in most cases quite unspecific and not directed to the surgeon—being irritable, snappy, disliking people more, not being able to stand scenes in the movies where violence was displayed, etc.

The second stage of our interest occurred when the surgeons had to deal with a large number of people after the Coconut Grove fire in Boston who had severe burns and would not cooperate. They were very angry with their well-meaning surgeons, kicked the nurses away, tore off their transplantations and their infusions, and were just nasty patients. On inspection it turned out that those people who were upset in this manner were people who were confronted with death, but not their own: They were afraid that their wife or husband, as the case might be, had been caught in the fire; often they didn't yet know what had happened. They had a high level of uncertainty, and they were concerned with the flood of imagery which comes to the griever about somebody lost.

We then had an opportunity to study what a grieving person does. One of these grievers, before we had learned how to help them, jumped out of a window. It turned out that he wanted to be with his wife. Other patients then gave us a whole variety of the basic ingredients of the grief process. And only when we helped them to do their grieving—once they knew with certainty that the loved one has died in the fire—were we able to make it possible for them to be as cooperative with their physician as I guess I have been here!

Now, what did one have to watch for? This confrontation with death meant induced rage: Who has been the villain? "Was I the villain? I should not have taken my wife to that club. Somebody should have seen that there were proper protections against the fire"—and so on. First, accusations. Accusations, we learned later, often go against the surgeon who lost the patient or against the funeral director. So, increased hostility. Second, waves of sorrow and preoccupation with the image of the deceased. This image was often very disturbing—for instance, being in the fire or trying to help the person who is about to die in the fire. A variety of images in one's mind—and really, one of the worst pains there is, is sorrow. Having to suffer this, one gradually masters this pain, and gradually gets away from the inclination one has not to think about it, to be busy with getting the deceased out of one's mind—forgetting it—putting things away which belonged to him; moving into another place so that one will not be reminded of him. Or, one is busy with this aggression against people, looking for the villain but avoiding thinking of the patient. On the other hand, one may suffer through his mourning, and while one does that, do the essentials of grief work, which now becomes important for all people who are faced with a loss, including *losing themselves.*

This grief work has to do with the effort of reliving and working through in small quantities events which involved the now-deceased person and the survivor: the things one did together, the roles one had vis-à-vis each other, which were complementary to each other and which one would pass through day by day in the day's routine. Each item of this shared role has to be thought through, *pained* through, if you want, and gradually the question is raised, How can I do that with somebody else? And gradually the collection of activities which were put together in this unit with the person who has died can be torn asunder and be put onto other people. So it can be divided among other future role partners, who then become loved a little—not much, perhaps, at first—but become tolerable, with whom one can do things and have companionship.

This process is something which can be learned. This one can see some people do well, while others never learn it. If they don't learn it they often remain stuck in this early period of grieving, in the first phase of the grief process, in which one has a global relationship to the person lost—perhaps in heaven, perhaps in a picture on the wall. One speaks or prays to that image, sets a place for the person as an imaginary companion at the breakfast table, speaks to the children as if the person was still there, and cannot abandon the total image in favor of partial relationships to parts of this person.

Now I began with parts, when I spoke of losing one's uterus, rather than losing one's whole person. And I think it is important to keep in mind that this problem of relationship to a total entity of a person as compared to partial aspects of his doing, or to parts of his or one's own body, is one of the major themes which occurs in people who are confronted with impending death and who have in their body a dangerous tumor—or, for that matter, have had a heart attack or an amputation of the leg, lose their eyes, etc. In each of these situations, the "job," what we call *grief work,* arises: to think out the aspects of the new role which one has to play in life. With our uterus-deprived women, the question of a new sexual role arises: will I be a cold partner to my husband, or will he think I am, even if I'm not? And so the sexual role relationship threatens to be altered, has to be worked through, and often is neglected to be worked through. The person who loses a leg and has to be rehabilitated has to learn the role of a legless fellow, who will be received by other people in new role constellations—which must be acceptable to him and to the other persons because one of the ingredients of comfortable living is to have a reference group that accepts one's identity and accepts that network of roles in which one relates to them.

And so in a variety of medical events, which are witnessed by various departments, this process of grieving and of learning new roles takes place, and has to be achieved if one wants to be a mentally healthy griever. Out of this study of grief arose what is now called *community mental health,* where, instead of waiting for illnesses, one tries to find people who are in grief states in response to losses of various kinds, including medical losses, and helps them with these processes. This work is a form of preventive psychiatry or preventive medicine. If they get stuck in this process without knowing it, people then find themselves in a condition of being neurotics, or often psychotics, or angry, ugly persons whom nobody likes. They then become the patients from whom one turns away in the ward, to whom one doesn't talk, and who are so unpleasant and hostile that the social network which is necessary, on the ward perhaps more than in a good many other places, cannot be reestablished with them.

The patient who is caught in the confrontation with a severe impending loss, in this case of his own self, and who has to do *anticipatory grieving,* as we call it now, is facing a psychological job, which can be facilitated by those who look after him or be impeded inadvertently because one doesn't know what is going on; and so one comes out with some of the casualties of maladaptive grief processes. They then have to be handled one way or the other, and usually one is very unhappy with these people.

Now let us turn away from partial losses and think about losing of oneself in threatening death. Some time left, a little time left, a long time left?—how much, one doesn't know. How many impeding aspects are there in the situation? And one of the big things is uncertainty, as it was with our burn patients— the uncertainty about the timing of one's own loss. The problem then is the reaching out and clamoring for information from the physician that he often cannot give. One of the tensions between the patient and yourselves is that you cannot give the information which he wants and which in some way you really ought to be able to give him; but you have a lot of misgivings about giving him that. I went through this in a very big way indeed with my illness and the threat in my system. And so it is a matter of knowledge: information seeking is an essential part of the mentally healthy effort of adapting to a crisis situation.

Around this matter of information getting so many issues have arisen that a whole book has been written about it by Anselm Strauss, a sociologist, and a nurse friend of his. They write in great detail, having studied various hospitals, about the habitual "culture pattern" of communication of the doctors, nurses, and social workers vis-à-vis one another, the patient, and the family. The problem is what information to give to whom, to avoid contradictory information to different participants in a social orbit. Problems arise such as who ought to be the bearer of good or bad news. The relevant participants in this social orbit are likely to receive opposing messages, and the patient is confronted with contradictory information. Then his task is not to adapt to information, period!—but to figure out what is right and what is wrong. And so information getting and transmission is one of the important things.

The second thing is, what does one do with sorrow, the bad feelings? Patients who are confronted with impending loss are busy with weeping, with painful experiences; and there is an inclination in many medical cultures to consider the good patient as a brave patient, who doesn't show any misery and who—you might almost say—is nice to the doctor by not showing how upset he is because he doesn't want to make his friend the doctor upset. This is a very common reaction among patients. And so the problem is, how does one deal with the masses of emotion? Well, the important thing is that emotions can be displayed and emotions can be shared. Often the nurses are the ones who are the most skillful in this, in sharing the emotions, and who, however, then need a little backing from *their* friends in their social orbit when they go through too much of that. The nurses in the intensive-care unit are especially endangered in that way, with such an immediate threat of death. And all these things happen very rapidly, over and over again, and they need help. For instance, in some of the intensive-care units we now have nurses' groups, in which they tell each other about feelings such as "I killed that patient—I didn't watch out at the right moment," and that sort of thing, this sense of guilt about not having been properly available or not having used the right judgment. And so the problem of

emotions arising and being displayed has to do not only with
the patient but also with the caretaking staff: doctor, nurse,
social worker, etc.—with their responses and with their sharing, with the patient and with their colleagues, and with
themselves. And this emotional impact is a job to be done
which takes time. Grieving, if there is a really dear person, takes
six weeks. And if you have to come to terms with your own
demise, it also takes time.

A number of studies have now been done under the heading
of terminal care, trying to figure out carefully what is the mode
by which this job is done by patients under various circumstances. How is it different in the case of mentally healthy
versus neurotic patients, and what devices does one learn from
one patient that one can give to another patient. This matter of
learning from sufferers and communicating with new sufferers
about it has now become a part of psychiatry called *research on
coping*. How do people cope with stress situations, such as
impending death? And how can one tell other people confronted with such stress how it has been done by successful
persons? And how can the means be taught most effectively?

Now, what sort of things have I, for instance, learned, and
which did I use in my own coping? One thing which impressed
me very much was a book by Hans Zinsser, who was a faculty
member at Stanford some years ago—a man who died of
leukemia at a relatively young age, when he thought he had
only done about a third of what he was going to do. He had to
grieve about himself. Since grieving means to review shared
experiences, he reviewed those experiences which he had had
with Hans Zinsser! He looked him up very carefully, and
reconstructed his life, and out of this came one of the most
fascinating books, called *As I Remember Him*. In it he describes this partly idealized, partly odd sort of person who was
that wonderful guy Hans! Putting him there and loving him—
and perhaps sometimes while he was writing, sorrowing a

lot—he came to terms with the fact that this *was* once, and lives in memory, but in the future will not be there as an identity. It can only be represented by symbols, such as a book, or—there is a building named for me in Boston, the Lindemann Mental Health Center, which means an awful lot. So you have something which continues your identity's existence by a global attribute, a book or a building which then allows the survivors to remember those things which are pertinent to *you,* the particular person, just as at various stages of your anticipatory grieving you think about various aspects of that life which you are now reconstructing.

Now the reading of this book was a revelation to me and led me to wonder, in looking at grief patients, if they have similar tasks? They don't write books, but with members of their families, or the nurse, they have confidential exchanges about the sort of things they did with other people. They like to be visited by a lot of friends, as long as they don't feel too embarrassed about their emotions, and would like to pick up items in their lives which they shared with the future survivors. And they will rub in these experiences with the family and friends, so that they will be sure to remember when they are gone. So this constructing a collective surviving image of oneself which still will be there when one happens not to be there any more in the flesh is the core of grieving, which, if it is done well, is apt to become an admirable process—a fascinating process if one is lucky enough to witness it.

And every once in a while one hears about some person who is confronted with a severe illness and is not going to live, who is an inspiration to somebody else. And from our observations, it is these people who do such a good job of recalling their own lives and their own shared experiences, constructing an image which is a tenable image of a human being.

Now if that is so, one can understand why in books dealing with terminal care, the authors are concerned that there is not enough contact between the patient and his family. The family gets into a conflict over whether to stay or not, how much to share in the patient's illness; whether these sometimes trite things which the patient brings up are worth the time of the patient and everybody else. And for the family, a very important problem may come up, which may have been mentioned here by David Kaplan and Dr. Fishman in connection with the mothers of leukemic children—namely, that one does one's grieving so well that one emancipates oneself from the person who is going to die and then has no relationship any more. The parents don't know whether to visit or whether to stay away; if they try to pull themselves out of the bondage they will feel they are disloyal. This problem of a relationship which may be severed too successfully becomes a difficult one for the anticipatory griever. Sometimes patients who have a terminal illness come to terms with this illness, are all settled; and then when people still come, they don't want to see them any more. One wonders what is the matter with them unless one is aware of the fact that a process has been going on, and one has to tap at what phase this process now is.

The next point is the problem of the model for this new kind of endeavor, coming to terms with one's own death. How have other people done it? Does one know somebody who was a good terminal patient? Therefore, the need to know other patients, knowing other people in a similar predicament, becomes so important. That's why some departments have developed groups of patients who meet each other, and why I found the experience in your waiting room helpful, where we got together in our funny little gowns and where you can see the typical evolution of a group process. People when they first come there are very stiff, they don't talk, "they really aren't sick but have just come in order to be irradiated"; finally someone dares to speak about leukemia; what a remarkable place this department is compared to other clinics where they may have been treated; *they* don't know yet what's wrong, but *they* are surely going to find out. So they are proud of the place, and having something to be proud of, they gradually begin to be proud of themselves, telling each other what good patients they are. And a little later, the problem is, can they tell each other what good grievers they are, and how they can come to terms with their death. That comes only after quite a while; it is likely to come first in a dyadic relationship; with a nurse or with a doctor whom one trusts. On the other hand, the learning from a model, perhaps doing it better than a model who doesn't do so well—that's the kind of thing one can have only in a group. And that is where the information we have assembled in psychiatry about group process is very important here, in this particular section of general medicine.

Having a model, then, for the grief process is the third item one hopes will be successfully managed in the person exposed to this need in his life. If it is done successfully, we rejoice with the patient; if he fails to do it, we hope there will be somebody who knows this sort of thing. And we have made great efforts to have not only psychiatrists but also our medical colleagues and our clergymen, who are often the persons chosen as communicators by physicians, know some of these aspects. I think I years? Then it really hits you, and the thing that hits you is that the items in it, and the point that it is not just a naughty patient, or one who doesn't know what it is all about, but a patient who is caught up in not knowing how to do a certain psychological task.

Now I'm sure you don't often have a patient who is also a physician and a psychiatrist and who went through this, and so I shall say a little about some of these items of the work which indeed I have done somewhere, otherwise I couldn't talk with ease about it. They happened to align themselves in confrontation with a chordoma, one of the worst forms of tumor, which was discovered during an exploratory operation three years too late, having been misdiagnosed for three years as a virus or a disc. The surgeon, when he came to send me to radiation, saying he couldn't remove it, was so unhappy that *I* had to comfort *him*, that he had missed the boat. And he said, well, you have three or four years now, can you do with three or four years? Then it really hits you, and the thing that hits you is that you are not immortal. Because there is a curious conviction in some way in everybody that one is immortal. We can't really imagine ourselves dead. When you dream about death, you dream you are a perceiving dead person, and not a person who is nonexistent. And so you search for an image of what that is. There is a story about three clergymen who decided to check with each other, being sure that they would come back after three days; and one of them, being resurrected somehow, is supposed to tell his friends how it was, but all he can report is "totaliter aliter"—absolutely different!

And so one has to recoil from the nonexistence—and then say, what existence? Then the Zinsser model comes to one's mind—namely, the existence is the memory of the person who one was. One thinks back about the past, like mad! All the childhood experiences, boyhood experiences. I began to recall German poems I had memorized, and in terms of this poetry, relive past experiences. And as an older person looks back to an earlier period, just as Goethe in *Faust* looks back to the Ur-Faust, when he was a young man, he sees that that self which was there was interacting with other people than I do now, and I really am a chain of selves; one of them I am now, and in the future there will probably be just an agglomeration of these selves in the memory of other people.

And the next thing I did, which was so important for me as an anticipatory griever, was to actually look at the places of former experiences. I went to Germany and visited the places where I had grown up, the house of my birth; tried to find some people whom I had known then; went back to Heidelberg where I started my career; and did something which I should have done if I had stayed in Heidelberg instead of coming to the United States—that is, I gave a lecture to the medical students. It seemed important to make up for this opportunity which had been missed and which might not occur again. This making up for missed opportunities is a very important element, which anticipatory grievers can't do if they don't know they are going to die. As one knows from grief studies, unrelieved hostile relationships and quarrels which have not been redeemed are just as difficult an aspect of grieving as loving relationships which have led to a great attachment and a great loss of instinctual fulfillment. And therefore, getting quarrels straightened out with the people who are concerned is good not only for oneself who goes, but also for the people who stay afterwards. And to allow some people to have a fight with some of their relatives, maybe on the ward or in an appropriate room when they are in this particular period of life, rather than think "I must stop this right away and intervene" is a good thing to know.

And so, after dealing with the past and the present, the next thing is to get somehow a structure of the remaining future. Now that is where doctor, nurse, and the patient have to be so much together. So often you don't know exactly what to say. The problem is, how can you formulate the future in such a way that it is emotionally tolerable, that it is possible still to do certain things, and that there is an acceptable image of what happens after I am gone—that the people who are left over will have a tolerable life without me. What happens to the other people's grieving after I am gone, and what happens to the empty spot in the social system. Parents who leave children want to know how their children will grieve about them; what happens with the particular job and the particular income— that's where the social worker comes in—and with the particular place which one happens to have had as a buffer person between other people in a complicated social system. For example, one may have felt quite sure "that as long as I am there nothing can go wrong with the others." So one has to straighten that out. In other words, there has to be an opportunity to think about, recollect, and then enact those scenes which are unfinished business.

I really became hypomanic, in the sense that I raced around and wanted to do all the things that would be wonderful to do once more. In other words, see that people who are confronting death are not in an environment which is restrictive of *doing* possibilities; that they are still as mobile as is compatible with their ailments, and still as rich in possible experiences for a little while. I guess it isn't silly to make up for the things you won't have any more of later, and token fulfillment along that line can make an enormous difference.

These are the things to be worked at; and one can be a knowledgeable accomplice in this, as doctor, nurse and social worker, or one can stand there and be baffled: Why is the patient so ununderstandable? If the patient feels that you don't understand him, of course he often won't do certain aspects of his share of the treatment. Now one serious difficulty is that in an institution you don't have any time—I was amazed at how much time you people were able to take with me—and don't have the emotional resources to think of the patient as a suffering person who is going to die and lose himself, rather than as a specimen of a biological species with certain impairments which I luckily am able to fix up to a certain extent. "Maybe he, in my statistics, isn't one of the lucky ones, but I have a lot more who gradually can make up for him." Only "biological statistics" doesn't work for the patient; that is one of the things which requires an awful lot of altruism on the part of the patient who is just now very busy with narcissistic endeavors. But I think that once one understands this process, one can be surprised at how little actual time expenditure is needed to say the right word at the right time, and not too much; the right kind of affirmation that one accepts the patient with his particular style of coping; and in doing so forms what we call a therapeutic alliance with the patient—a companionship with the patient in the effort which he is making, rather than having him as the target of our ministrations.

BIOGRAPHICAL DATA

Family
Born May 2, 1900, in Witten, a town in the Ruhr valley, Germany. Second oldest of five children of Ernst Lindemann, a coal merchant, and his wife, Anna Raeker Lindemann.

Marriages:
Baldura Schmidt, Iowa City, 1929-1939
Elizabeth Brainerd, Dover, Massachusetts, 1939

Children: Adopted Jeffrey Ernst, born March 4, 1942 and Brenda, born July 8, 1944.

Death: November 16, 1974, following a long illness (malignant chordoma)

Education
Elementary school in Witten; Goethe Gymnasium in Essen. University of Marburg, 1919-1920.

University of Giessen, Ph.D. 1922; M.D., 1926. Studied Gestalt psychology with K. Koffka.

Postgraduate Training

Internships
  Hospital of Cologne Medical College, 1925
  University of Heidelberg, 1926-27
Resident Physician, Department of Neurology, University of Heidelberg, under V. von Weizsaecker, 1927

Research Associate in Experimental Psychology and Speech Pathology, University of Iowa, 1927-29.

Research Fellow in Physiology and Psychiatry, Rockefeller Foundation Fellowship, Harvard University, 1935-36.

Personal analysis
  Begun with Paul Schilder, 1932
  Completed with Helene Deutsch, 1941

Positions Held

University of Iowa
  Instructor in Psychology, 1929-31
  Assistant Professor in Psychology and Psychiatry, 1931-35
  Assistant Physician, University of Iowa Psychopathic Hospital, 1929-35
  Physician in Charge of Psychiatric Out-Patient Clinic, 1932-34

Massachusetts General Hopsital
  Assistant in Psychiatry, 1936-38
  Associate Psychiatrist and Physician-in-Charge, Psychiatric Out-Patient Department, 1938-46
  Consulting Psychiatrist, Massachusetts Eye and Ear Infirmary, 1943-65

Psychiatrist, 1946-54
Psychiatrist-in-Chief, Department of Psychiatry, 1954-65
Chairman of General Executive Committee, 1964-65

Harvard Medical School
  Instructor in Psychiatry, 1937-41
  Associate in Psychiatry, 1941-48
  Professor of Psychiatry, 1954-65
  Professor of Psychiatry, Emeritus, 1965-74

Harvard School of Public Health
  Instructor in Psychiatry, 1940-41
  Lecturer on Mental Health, 1948-51
  Associate Professor of Mental Health, 1951-54

Harvard University Department of Social Relations
  Lecturer in Clinical Psychology and Psychiatry, 1947-53

Human Relations Service of Wellesley, Inc.
  Medical Director, 1949-65

Boston Psychoanalytic Institute
  Lecturer in Psychoanalysis, 1944-50

Stanford University Medical School
  Visiting Professor of Psychiatry, 1965-74

Boston College
  Visiting Professor of Psychiatry in the Department of Psychology, 1968-72

Offices and Memberships
American Psychiatric Association
  Chairman, Committee on Preventive Psychiatry, 1952

American Psychosomatic Society
  Member of Executive Council, 1954

Boston Psychoanalytic Society
  President, 1943-46

Group for the Advancement of Psychiatry
  Chairman, Committee on Preventive Psychiatry, 1950-53

National Institute of Mental Health
  Member of Mental Health Study Section on Public Health
    Programs, 1951-66
  Member, Committee on Social and Physical Environment
    Variables as Determinants of Mental Health (Leonard
    Duhl's "Space Cadets,") 1955-62

National Research Council
  Member of Committee on Stress, 1951-54

Commonwealth of Massachusetts
  Member of Advisory Committee on Mental Health Plan-
    ning, 1962-65

Social Science Research Council
  Member of Committee on Social Psychiatry, 1949-53

Services at the International Level
World Health Organization
  Member, Expert Advisory Panel to Mental Health Section,
    1952-67
  Chairman, Study Group on Ataractic and Hallucinogenic
    agents, 1957
  Special Consultant to study the development of psychiatric
    education in Indian Medical Colleges, 1959

Lindauer Psychotherapie Wochen
Faculty member, 1959-72 Leader of Selbsterfahrungs Group, 1962-72

University of Tuebingen
Visiting Professor of Social Psychiatry, summer semester, 1966

University of Heidelberg
Consultant to Social Psychiatry Program, 1968-71

International Congress of Social Psychiatry, London, Vice-president, 1964

Conference on Mental Health Research in Asia and the Pacific, Honolulu, 1966
Generalist consultant

Honors

The General Court of the Commonwealth of Massachusetts designated the Mental Health Center in the Government Center, Boston, as the Erich Lindemann Mental Health Center, January, 1970. Dedication ceremonies were held on September 22, 1971.

Organizations conferring honorary or life membership, or certificates of appreciation include
American Psychiatric Association
Deutsche Gesellschaft fuer Psychiatrie und Nervenheilkunde
Indian Psychiatric Society
Mental Health Section of the American Public Health Association

Massachusetts Psychological Association
National Institute of Mental Health
Psychiatric Outpatient Centers of America

THE WORKS OF
ERICH LINDEMANN

1922

Experimentelle Untersuchungen ueber das Entstehen und Vergehen von Gestalten. *Psychiatrische Forschung* 1:34–88.

1926

Untersuchungen ueber primitive Intelligenzleistungen hochgradig Schwachsinniger u. ihr Verhaeltnis zu den Leistungen von Anthropoiden. *Zeitschrift fur die gesamte Neurologie und Psychiatrie* 104:529–569.

1929

Alteration of the action current of skeletal muscles following sympathetic ramisection (with A. Steindler). *Journal of Bone and Joint Surgery* 11:1–9.

1930

Studies of action currents in laryngeal nerves. *Proceedings of the Society for Experimental Biology and Medicine* 27:249–480.

1931

The psychopathological effect of sodium amytal. *Proceedings of the Society for Experimental Biology and Medicine* 28:864–866.

1932

Psychological changes in normal and abnormal individuals under the influence of sodium amytal. *American Journal of Psychiatry* 11:1080–1091.

1933

The dynamics of psychiatric reaction-type determination (with W. Malamud). *American Journal of Psychiatry* 13:347–367.

Effects of alcohol on the chronaxia of the motor system (with W. Malamud and H.H. Jasper). *Archives of Neurology and Psychiatry* 29:790.

1934

Experimental analysis of the psychopathological effects of intoxicating drugs. *American Journal of Psychiatry* 13:983–1006.

The neurophysiological effect of intoxicating drugs (with W. Malamud and H.H. Jasper). *American Journal of Psychiatry* 13:1007–1037.

1935

The psychopathological effect of drugs affecting the vegetative system: 1. adrenalin. *American Journal of Psychiatry* 91:993–1008.

1938

Hysteria as a problem a general hospital. *Medical Clinics of North America,* Boston Number, May pp. 591–605.

The effect of adrenalin and mecholyl in states of anxiety in psychoneurotic patients (with J. Finesinger). *American Journal of Psychiatry* 95:353–370.

1940
The subjective response of psychoneurotic patients to adrenalin and mecholyl (with J. Finesinger). *Psychosomatic Medicine* 2:231–248.

1941
Observations on psychiatric sequelae to surgical operations in women. *American Journal of Psychiatry* 98:132–139. [chapter 1, this volume]

1942
Clinical implications of measurements of interaction rates in psychiatric interviews (with E.D. Chapple). *Applied Anthropology* 1:1–11.

Therapeutic procedure in psychoneurosis. *New England Journal of Medicine* 227:584–589.

1943
Neuropsychiatric observations after the Coconut Grove fire (with S. Cobb). *Annals of Surgery* 117:814–824. [abbreviated version appears as chapter 3, this volume]

1944
Symptomatology and management of acute grief. *American Journal of Psychiatry* 101:141–148. [chapter 4, this volume]

1945
A discussion of the psychiatric aspects of rehabilitation (with J. Finesinger). *Diseases of the Nervous System* 6:1–8.

Psychiatric aspects of the conservative treatment of ulcerative colitis. *Society Transactions, Archives of Neurology and Psychiatry* 53:322–325.

1946
Autonomic nervous system. In *Encyclopedia of Psychology*, ed. P.L. Harriman, pp. 48–56. New York: Philosophical Library.

Psychotherapeutic opportunities for the general practitioner. *Bulletin of the New England Medical Center* 8:6, December.

1947
Effect of anoxia as measured by the electroencephalogram and the interaction chronogram on psychoneurotic patients (with J. Finesinger, M.A.B. Brazier, and E.D. Chapple). *New England Journal of Medicine* 236:783–793.

Dwarfism in healthy children: its possible relation to emotional, nutritional, and endocrine disturbances (with N.B. Talbot et al.). *New England Journal of Medicine* 236:783–793.

1949
Individual hostility and group integration. *Human Organism* 8:5–9. [chapter 5, this volume]

A university psychiatric hospital. *Human Organism* 8:10–12.

Social science in relation to medicine and some of its recent contributions. *Cincinnati Journal of Medicine* 30:475–481.

1950
Emotional maturity (with Ina M. Greer). *Journal of Pastoral Care* 3:1–11.

Epidemiological aspects of minor mental disorders. (with J. Gordon, W. Vaughan, and J. Ipsen) In *Epidemiology of Mental Disorder,* pp. 11–35. New York: Milbank Memorial Fund.

An epidemiological analysis of suicide. (with J. Gordon, J. Ipsen, and W. Vaughan). In *Epidemiology of Mental Disorder,* pp. 136–175. New York: Milbank Memorial Fund

Modifications in the course of ulcerative colitis in relationship to changes in life situations and reaction patterns. *Life Stress and Bodily Disease,* Association for Research in Nervous and Mental Disorders, 29:706–723. [chapter 2, this volume]

Human Relations Study in Wellesley. *Massachusetts Health Journal 31:5–7.*

1951
Psychiatry. *Annual Review of Medicine* 2:219–224.

Medicine as a science: psychiatry. Part of the series, "Fifty Years of Medical Progress." *New England Journal of Medicine* 244:729–762.

1952
The biological and social sciences in an epidemiology of mental disorder (with J. Gordon, E. O'Rourke, and F.L.W. Richardson). *American Journal of the Medical Sciences* 223:316–343.

Modifications in ego structure and personality reactions under the influence of the effects of drugs (with L.D. Clark). *American Journal of Psychiatry* 108–561–567.

The role of medical education in modern society. *American Journal of Psychiatry* 109:89–92.

Early stresses and strains of marriage (with Ina M. Greer). *Pastoral Psychology* 2:10–13.

Use of psychoanalytic constructs in preventive psychiatry. Part 1. *Psychoanalytic Study of the Child* 7:429–437. [portions revised and included in chapter 7, this volume]

1953
Mental health: fundamental to a dynamic epidemiology of health. In *Epidemiology of Health*, pp. 109–124. New York: Health Education Council. [chapter 6, this volume]

Die Bedeutung emotionaler Zustaende fuer das Verstaendnis mancher innerer Krankheiten und ihre Behandlung. Translated by C. Benda. *Die Medizinische,* Nr. 15 u. 18, 11 April u. 2 Mai.

The Wellesley Project for the study of certain problems in community mental health. In *Interrelations between the Social Environment and Psychiatric Disorders,* pp. 167–186. New York: Milbank Memorial Fund. [portions revised and included in chapter 7, this volume]

A study of grief: emotional responses to suicide. (with Ina M. Greer) *Pastoral Psychology,* December, pp. 9–13.

1955
Preventive intervention in a four-year-old child whose father committed suicide (with W. Vaughan, Jr., and M. McGinnis). *Emotional Problems of Early Childhood,* ed. G. Caplan, pp. 5–30. New York: Basic Books.

Psychiatry service, 1954–1955. *The News,* Masschusetts General Hospital 147:1–2.

Interprofessional relationships. *Annals of the New York Academy of Science* 63:338–340.

The medical psychological dynamics of the gamut of normal experiences of the normal individual. In *Ministry and Medicine in Human Relations,* pp. 16–32. New York: International Universities Press.

1956
The meaning of crisis in individual and family living. *Teachers College Record* 57:310–315.

Brief psychotherapy of a patient with headache and endometriosis. *American Journal of Medicine* 20:286–291, 1956. [record of a case discussion]

A family study unit. In *Changing Concepts of Psychoanalytic Medicine,* ed. S. Rado and G.E. Daniels, pp. 162–164. New York: Grune and Stratton.

1957
The nature of mental health work as a professional pursuit. In *Psychology and Mental Health,* appendix A, C.R. Strother, pp. 136–145. American Psychological Association.

The psychosocial position on etiology. In *Integrating the Approaches to Mental Disease,* ed. H.D. Kruse, pp. 34–39. New York: Hoeber-Harper.

Problems related to grandparents. In *Understanding Your Patient,* ed. S. Liebman, pp. 147–158. Philadelphia and Montreal: Lippincott.

Psychiatry department. *The News,* Massachusetts General Hospital 164.

1958

Hallucinations of poliomyelitis patients during treatment in a respirator (with J. Mendelson and P. Solomon). *Journal of Nervous and Mental Diseases* 126:421–428.

1959

The relation of drug-induced mental changes to psychoanalytic theory. *Bulletin of the World Health Organization* 21:8–14.

1960

The mental health educator and the community. In *Mental Health Education: A Critique* pp. 51–64. Philadelphia: Pennsylvania Mental Health, Inc.

Psychiatric activities in general hospitals. *Medical Education Bulletin* 5:8–14. New Delhi: Patiala House.

Feldstudien in der vorbeugenden Psychiatrie. *Praxis der Psychotherapie* 5:22–23.

Background factors related to psychosocial development. The ingredients of personality. In *The Healthy Child*, ed. H.D. Stuart and D.C. Prugh, pp. 192–202. Cambridge: Harvard University Press.

Critical ages for maternal bereavement in psychoneuroses (with H. Barry). *Psychosomatic Medicine* 22:166–181.

Psychosocial factors as stressor agents. In *Stress and Psychiatric Disorders*, ed. J.M. Tanner, pp. 13–17. Oxford: Blackwell Scientific Publications.

1961

Sociocultural factors in mental health and illness (with M. Fried). *American Journal of Orthopsychiatry* 31:86–101.

Nursing's contribution to psychiatry. (part of article, Nursing's contribution to a famous hospital). *Nursing Outlook* 9.

Die soziale Organisation der menschlichen Lebewesen. *Praxis der Psychotherapie* 2:49–62.

Newcomers' problems in a suburban community (with L. Thoma). *Journal of the American Institute of Planners* 3 (27): 185–193. [portions revised and included in chapter 8, this volume]

Preventive intervention in individual and family crisis (with D. Klein). In *Prevention of Mental Disorders in Children,* ed. G. Caplan, pp. 283–307. New York: Basic Books.

Drug effects and personality theory (with J.M. von Felsinger). *Psychopharmacologia* 2:69–92.

Recent studies on preventive intervention in social and emotional crises. In *Recent Research Looking toward Preventive Intervention,* ed. R.H. Ojemann, pp. 10–40. Ames, Iowa: State University of Iowa.

1962

Beobachtungen ueber Krankheiten and psychische Reaktionen in verschiedenen Gelsellschaftsshichten und Kulturen. *Der Internist* 3, (2):72–76.

Die Vorbeugung psychosomatischer Erkrankungen mit Rucksicht auf den sozialen Raum. *Praxis der Psychotherapie* 7 4:166–173.

Preventive intervention in situational crises. In *Clinical Psychology,* ed. G.S. Nielsen, pp. 69–80. Copenhagen: Munksgaard. [chapter 10, this volume]

1963

Mental health and the environment. In *The Urban Condition,* ed. L.D. Duhl. pp. 3–10. New York: Basic Books.

Grief. In *The Encyclopedia of Mental Health,* vol. 1, ed., A. Deutsch and H. Fishman, pp. 703–76. New York: Franklin Watts.

Human growth and development in a world of chronic crisis. In *Transactions of Conference on Human Services.* Harrisburg: Commonwealth of Pennsylvania.

1964

A foundation for preventive practice in child psychiatry. In *Preventive Child Psychiatry,* ed., D.A. Van Krevelen, pp. 30–40. Berne, Switzerland: Hans Huber.

Adolescent behavior as a community concern. *American Journal of Psychotherapy* 18:405–417.

Current concepts of prevention in mental health. In *The Proceedings of the Conference on the Role of Mental Health in Settlement and Community Centers,* Massachusetts Department of Mental Health.

Some psychological aspects of subcultures in disadvantaged areas. In *Education in Disadvantaged Urban Areas.* School Document No. 7, pp. 84–94. Boston: Boston Public Schools.

1965

The health needs of communities. In *Hospitals, Doctors, and the Public Interest,* ed., J. Knowles, pp. 271–292. Cambridge: Harvard University Press.

Crises in family life. *Annual Proceedings of Conference and*

Institute, ed., D.N. Cannon, pp. 13–20. Child Association of America.

Social system factors as determinants of resistance to change. *American Journal of Orthopsychiatry* 35:544–556.

Sucht und Rausch als Krankheit. *Muenchener medizinische Wochenschrift,* 107 (49):2461–2466. [portions revised and included in chapter 9, this volume]

Mental health services relating to crises in urbanization. In *Die Begegnung mit dem kranken Menschen.* ed., A. Friedemann, pp. 75–90. Berne and Stuttgart: Hans Huber.

The timing of psychotherapy. *The Sixth International Congress of Psychotherapy: Selected Lectures,* pp. 75–90. Basel, New York: S. Karger. [with one or two minor changes, text is identical with Preventive intervention in situational crises, 1962]

Transition in psychiatry: Dr. Lindemann retires. *The News,* Massachusetts General Hospital 24(6):2–7.

1966

Dependency in adult patients following early maternal bereavement (with H. Barry, Jr. and H. Barry, III). *Journal of Nervous and Mental Diseases* 140:196–206.

Community mental health services. *Work Conference in Graduate Education (Psychiatric) Mental Health Nursing.* pp. 9–13. University of Pittsburgh, School of Nursing.

1967

Die therapeutische Bedeutung derverbalen und nonverbalen Kommunikationsformen zwischen Aerzten und Patienten. *Praxis der Psychotherapie.* 7(1):24–31.

1969

Kulturwandel und Gweissen. *Muenchener medizinische Wochenschrift,* 111:27, 1010–1015 [a translation approved by the auther appears as chapter 12, this volume]

Mental health aspects of rapid social change. In *Mental Health Research in Asia and the Pacific*, ed. W. Caudill and Tsung-Yi Lin, pp. 478–487. Honolulu: East-West Center Press. [abbreviated version appears as chapter 11, this volume]

1971

Professional and community: pathways toward trust (with F.W. Ilfeld, Jr.). *American Journal of Psychiatry* 128(5):583–589.

1974

Coping with long-term disability (with J.E. Adams). *Coping and Adaptation,* ed. G.V. Coelho, D.A. Hamburg, and J.E. Adams, pp. 127–138. New York: Basic Books.

1976

Grief and grief management: some reflections. *Journal of Pastoral Care 30(3) 198–207.*

INTRODUCTIONS AND REVIEWS

1953

Social psychiatry. *Convergent Trends in Contemporary Psychiatry*, ed. F.F. Smith, New York.

1954

Review of *Furthering Mental Health in the Community,* H.L. Witner and R. Kotinsky.

1956

Preface to *Children and Other People,* R.S. Stewart and A.D. Workman. New York: Dryden Press.

1957

Preface to *Learning to Live as a Widow,* M. Langer, Gilbert.

1967

Review of *Short-term psychotherapy,* L.R. Wolberg. *International Journal of Group Psychotherapy.*

1968

Foreword to *Community Dynamics and Mental Health,* D.C. Klein. New York: Wiley.

1969

Introduction to *Distress in the City,* W. Ryan. Cleveland and London: Case Western Reserve.

1972

Geleitwort zu *Die therapeutische Gemeinschaft in der Psychotherapie und Sozialpsychiatrie,* A. Ploeger. Stuttgart: Georg Thieme, Verlag.

Index